看護医療系大学・短大・専門学校受験

石原式

会話で攻略！ メディカルイングリッシュ

石原　修

東京コア

はじめに

会話文は，慣用的表現を一通り覚えてしまえば取り組みやすい英文といえます。もちろん話題にされる内容にもよりますが，一般的には評論文や小説文などと比べればずっと読みやすいはずです。まして興味関心のある話題であれば，とっつきやすいのではないでしょうか。そのやさしい興味のある英文を使って文法もおぼえてしまおうというのが本書の狙いです。文法は，医療系入試で出題されるというだけでなく，英語の知識を増殖させていくためには不可欠な知識です。本書は入試英文法をすべて網羅しているわけではありませんが，医療系大学・短大受験志望者の皆さんにとっては必要にして最小限の内容といえます。わからない箇所があってもそこで投げないで，飛ばしてまずは読み通してみましょう。必ずしも問題形式で進める必要はまったくありません。何回転かするうちに内容が身についてくるものです。本書に触発されて英語学習にさらなるはずみがつけば幸いです。

私の好きな言葉にWhere there is a will, there is a way.というのがあります。「この世の中で願って叶わないことはない，それに向けて努力を重ねれば必ず道が開けてくる」といったような意味です。中学時代に英語の先生（湯原知一先生）から教わって，私の人生の要所要所で支えてくれている言葉です。これから医療系を目指される皆さんには，漠然とした願望ではなくて明確な目的意識をもって受験勉強に励んでもらいたいと思います。

Great minds have purposes, others have wishes.
（賢人は目的を，小人は願望をもつ）

本書の出版に関して快くお引き受けいただきました株式会社東京コアの竹田允彦氏また大杉研二氏に厚く御礼を申し上げます。さらに，執筆にあたり，友人のDavid Allen氏（米国人）に英文作成を，Tom Slavic氏（米国人）とRhian Yoshikawa氏（英国人）に英文校正で協力してもらいました。編集には小野裕紀子氏他多くの方々にご協力いただきました。ここに厚くお礼を申し上げます。

最後に，本書をお読みいただいた受験生が合格の栄冠をつかまれることを念願してやみません。

平成20年３月吉日

石原　修

CONTENTS

オリジナル問題

● 凡例 ●

名…名詞　動…動詞　形…形容詞　副…副詞　⇔…反意語　＝…同義語

COLUMN

本書の特徴と使いかた

本書は，**実力診断テスト**，**オリジナル問題30題**，**実戦入試過去問題10題**，**医療系によくでる英単語**から構成されています。その他コラムとして，「ことわざから学ぶ文法」や「意外な意味をもつ単語」さらに「医療系の慣用表現」などを掲載してあります。楽しみながら医療系入試英語と文法を学ぶことが可能です。また**オリジナル問題完全英文**は，音読用に利用できるようにしてあります。

●オリジナル問題〈英文〉●

テーマに沿った会話文の問題です。実力診断テストが12点以下の人は，正答と照らし合わせながら通読してみましょう。繰り返し最低３回読み通せば，知らず知らずのうちに入試会話文問題のパターンと表現が身につくはずです。13点以上の人は，まずは解いてみましょう。間違えた問題はきちんとチェックし，さらに表現集や英単語集からインプットに励みましょう。もし苦痛を感じるようなら，基礎からじっくり取り組むつもりで正答を見ながら通読方式に切り替えてください。

⬇

●オリジナル問題〈和訳〉●

英文問題の和訳を掲載しています。意訳しすぎず原文がわかるように訳してあります。英文と照らし合わせてください。語句解説を参照して理解を深めましょう。

⬇

●文法・語法／医療系の慣用表現●

各テーマで使われている文法・語法を解説しています。また，医療系でよく使われる慣用表現や言い回しなどを掲載しています。

⬇

●実戦入試過去問題●

オリジナル問題を解いたら，過去問題にチャレンジしましょう。実際の試験で出題された問題を解くことで，実戦に役立ちます。

⬇

●オリジナル問題完全英文／医療系によくでる英単語●

オリジナル問題の完全英文は，音読してみましょう。ただ目で眺めるだけでは，なかなか記憶にはとどまりません。五感を刺激することで，記憶力がアップします。

最後に医療系にでてくる英単語を掲載しています。英文読解に役立つ知識です。

まずは自分の実力をCHECK！

実力診断テスト

1 次のX，Yの会話で，空所に入る最も適したものをA～Dの中から１つ選び記号で答えなさい。（各１点）

(1) X : Will you be home on Sunday afternoon?

Y : ＿＿＿＿＿＿＿＿＿＿＿＿

A. I'm afraid of Sunday.　　B. I'm afraid I won't.

C. I certainly will be.　　D. I hope I will.

(2) X : I hate trains on a wet day like this.

Y : ＿＿＿＿＿＿＿＿＿＿＿＿

A. So do I.　　B. So am I.

C. Neither do I.　　D. Neither am I.

(3) X : Why don't you take a day off?

Y : ＿＿＿＿＿＿＿＿＿＿＿＿

A. Because I was.　　B. Good idea. I will.

C. How do you do?　　D. Neither am I.

2 次のA，Bの会話の意味が通るように（　）内に適当な語を入れなさい。ただし，〔　〕内の英語文とほぼ同じになるようにすること。（各１点）

(1) A : I appreciate your kindness.

B : (　　　) (　　　) it. 〔=You don't have to say that…〕

(2) A : (　　　) you. 〔=You can go first.〕

B : Oh, thank you.

(3) A : I didn't like the movie.

B : (　　　) come? 〔=Why?〕

3 次のイ，ロ，ハの会話の空所(1)～(3)に①～⑩の中から最も適切なものを選んで入れ会話を完成させなさい。（各１点）

イ. A : My car's broken down. Could you (1) to the station?

B : Sure get in.

ロ．A：Your new job seems wonderful. It sounds almost（　2　）.

B：Yes, that's what I thought, but it's a respectable company and I trust the boss.

ハ．A：Shall we go to a Chinese restaurant or have a pizza?

B：Either is OK. It's（　3　）.

① on your own　② make a comeback　③ up to you　④ give me a ride
⑤ hot item　⑥ too common　⑦ no danger of that　⑧ true to life
⑨ a sure thing　⑩ too good to be true

4 次の会話文の空所に入る最も適切な表現をイ～ニの中から選びなさい。（各１点）

A：I bet Donna likes you. Why don't you ask her out?

B：(　　　) I don't think she likes me at all.

イ．Give me a break.　ロ．Yes, that's a good idea.
ハ．Why is she out?　ニ．Come on, give it a try.

5 次の会話文の空所に入る最も適切な単語を（1）～（5）の中から選びなさい。

（各１点）

A：Hurray! We did it. At long last!

B：Yes, indeed. Our papers have been accepted. Isn't that（　　　）?

(1) everything　(2) nothing　(3) anything
(4) pretty little　(5) something

6 a，bの意味がほぼ同じになるように（　）内に適当な１語を入れなさい。（各１点）

(1) a. Will you do me a favor?
  b. May I（　　　）a favor of you?

(2) a. I don't want to eat anything now.
  b. I don't feel（　　　）eating anything now.

(3) a. May I trouble you for the butter?
  b.（　　　）me the butter, please.

(4) a. I am new to this neighborhood.
  b. I am a（　　　）around here.

解答・判定は次のページへ

実力診断テスト　解答と判定

●解答●

1 (1) B　(2) A　(3) B

2 (1) Don't mention　(2) After　(3) How

3 (1) ④　(2) ⑩　(3) ③

4 イ

5 (5)

6 (1) ask　(2) like　(3) Pass　(4) stranger

●判定●

15〜13点	かなりの実力がついています。さらに難しい問題にもチャレンジしていきましょう。
12〜8点	だいぶ実力がついていますが，もう一息です。会話の慣用表現のインプットに励みましょう。
7点以下	基礎がためが大事です。日々の積み上げが実力になります。

著者紹介

石原　修（いしはら　おさむ）

鹿児島県出身。現在大学非常勤講師，私塾主宰。早稲田大学卒業後ニューヨーク州立大学経営大学院修了（MBA）。都内大手予備校で長年大学受験生の英語を指導。超基礎レベルから帰国子女のハイレベルまで担当して受験生の悩み・つまずきを熟知している。現在，千葉県市川市内の私塾で中・高生の受験指導だけでなくTOEICやTOEFLの個別指導，留学相談も行っている。

オリジナル問題

30

A Cold
A Broken Leg
A Checkup
Chicken Pox
Insomnia
An Allergy
A Urine Test
A Check for Cancer
Blood Pressure
A Change of Hospital Rooms
A Medication Question
Teeth Cleaning
Visiting Hours
A Child Getting a Shot
A Bad Reaction to Medication
AIDS Warning to a Young Patient
The Flu
Dehydration
A Bad Cough
Doctor Referral (On the phone)
A Child's Dentist Appointment
Sleeping pills
Depression
A Blood Transfusion
An Emergency Call
A Medication Mistake
A Skin Problem
A First Visit
Weight Gain
Maternity

theme 1 A Cold

P : Patient　D : Doctor　Ph : Pharmacist

P : I've had a bad cold for a week.

D : Have you been taking anything (a) it?

P : Yes, but I don't feel any better.

D : (1) <u>Let's see if you have a fever</u> and I'll listen to your breathing.

(Later)

D : No fever. It's just a cold. This will help you get (b) it.

P : A prescription?

D : Yes. Have it (c), and take the medicine three times a day after meals.

(At the pharmacist)

Ph : (d). Take two capsules after breakfast, lunch and dinner.

P : For how long?

Ph : One week.

P : (2) <u>What if I don't feel better in a week?</u>

Ph : I think you will, but if not, call us and we can refill it for you.

P : Are there any side effects to this?

Ph : (3) (it, take, not, if, as, you, ordered). If you take it on an empty stomach, you might get a little drowsy.

設問 上の会話文を読んで次の設問に答えなさい。

1 下線部 (1) (2) を日本語に訳しなさい。

2 空所 (a) (b) に入る適切な前置詞を次の中から選びなさい。

① in　② on　③ over　④ at　⑤ to　⑥ for

3 空所 (c) に入る適語を次の中から選びなさい。

① fill　② filled　③ filling　④ to fill

4 空所 (d) には，なにか物を手渡すときの「はいどうぞ」という意味の文が入る。次の中から選びなさい。

① Here we go　② Here you are　③ Here I am

④ Here goes　　⑤ Here we are

5 (3) のカッコ内の単語を「指示されたように飲まないと（そうなりますよ）」という意味になるように並べ替えなさい。

語句解説

- I've had a bad cold for a week. ➡ have had は現在完了の継続用法「ずっと～している」「1週間ずっとひどい風邪をひいている」が直訳。
- I don't feel any better. の feel better は feel well「（身体）の調子がよい」の比較級。反対は feel bad「（身体）の調子が悪い」, feel good は「気分がいい，楽しい」の意味。ただし，この better は well でも good でも大した差はない。
- **I'll listen to your breathing.**　呼吸を聞いてみましょう。→ 聴診器をあててみましょう。➡ 聴診器は stethoscope，Let me use the stethoscope. ともいえる。
- **This will help you get over it.**　これはあなたが風邪を克服する手助けをするでしょう。→ これで風邪はよくなるでしょう。
  get over = **recover from**（病気など）から回復する
  get over a cold　風邪が治る
  help + O + (to) do　O が～する手助けをする，O が～するのに役立つ
- **prescription**　処方箋(せん)　動 **prescribe**　～を処方する
- Have it filled, and… ➡ この fill は「（処方箋）を調剤する」= fill out
  have＋O＋過去分詞「O を～してもらう」 it ＝処方箋
- take the medicine three times a day after meals
  この take は「（薬を）飲む，服用する」。drink にしないこと。
- Here you are. = Here you go. = Here it is. 「はいどうぞ」と物を差し出すときの表現。
- **What if ～?**　～したらどうなるだろうか
- in a week ➡ この in は時間の経過「～経って，～経ったら」を表す。
- **refill**　再調剤する　**refill it** = **represcribe the medicine**
- **side effect**　副作用　**Does it have any side effects?**　副作用ある？
- Not if you take it as ordered. = There aren't any side effects to this if you take it as you are ordered.
- **drowsy**　形 眠い，眠気を誘う

解答はp.13

テーマ 1 風 邪

患：患者　医者：医者　薬：薬剤師

患：ひどい風邪をひいてもう１週間になるんですけど。
医：なにか薬を飲んでいますか。
患：はい。でも全然よくならないんです。
医：熱があるか診てみましょう。聴診器をあててみます。
（しばらくして）
医：熱はありませんね。ただの風邪でしょう。これでよくなるでしょう。
患：処方箋ですね。
医：そうです。処方してもらってください。１日３回毎食後服用してください。
（薬局で）
薬：はいどうぞ。朝・昼・夕食後２錠ずつ服用してください。
患：どのくらい（の期間）ですか。
薬：１週間です。
患：１週間経ってよくならなかったらどうしたらいいですか。
薬：よくなると思いますが，もしよくならないようでしたら電話ください。補充します。
患：この薬はなにか副作用がありますか。
薬：指示通り服用すれば大丈夫です。空腹で服用すると眠くなるかもしれません。

解答

1 (1) 熱があるか診てみましょう。

(2) 1週間経ってよくならなかったらどうしたらいいでしょうか。

2 (a) ⑥　(b) ③

3 ②

4 ②

5 Not if you take it as ordered

解説

1 次のポイントを頭に入れて訳したい。

(1) see if ～「～かどうか調べてみる，見てみる」➡ この if は whether（～かどうか）の意で see, know, ask, wonder, tell, doubt などのあとで使う。

I wonder if you can help me with my homework.

宿題を手伝ってもらえるかしら。

(2) What if ～?「～したらどうなるだろうか」➡ この if は（もし～なら）で What if ～? は重要構文。

2

(a)「今ひいている風邪に対してなにか薬を飲んでいますか」だから for。

(b) get over「病気などを克服する，治す」の熟語から over を選ぶ。

3 fill は「処方箋を調剤する」。使役動詞 have は have + ㊚ + P.P.（過去分詞）という形で使うので filled を選ぶ。使役動詞の用法を含めて第 5 文型 SVOC は OC を SV に見立てて考えてみればおのずと C の形が決まる。たとえば，I heard my name called from behind.　後ろのほうから名前が呼ばれるのが聞こえた。／I heard someone call my name.　誰かが名前を呼ぶのが聞こえた。

4 **Here we go.**　さあ行くぞ。

Here I am.　ただ今帰りました。（＝**I'm home.**）／さあ着いた。

Here goes.　さあやるぞ。

Here we are.　さあ着いたぞ。／（欲しがっていた物が）さあここにありますよ。

5 省略があるためにわかりづらい問題かもしれない。文脈から次のようになる。

There are not any side effects to this if you take it as you are ordered.

文法 語法

■現在完了

基本的には，現在完了（have＋過去分詞）は過去のできごとが現在になんらかの影響を与えていることを示す表現形式。もう１度基本を確認しておきたい。

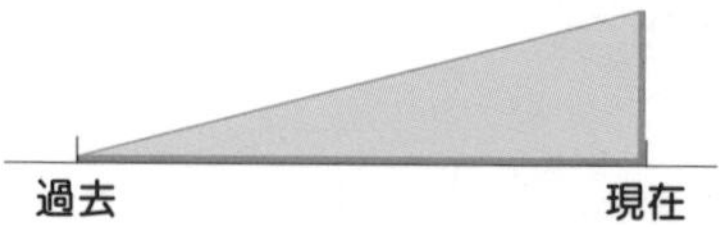

現在完了のイメージ図

4用法（4K）

経験（今までに～したことがある）

I have been to Australia twice.　オーストラリアに2回行ったことがあります。

I went to Australia. は単に過去の時点で行ったという事実を述べているだけだが，現在完了は行った経験が今に生きていると考えると違いがわかる。

継続（今までずっと～している）

I have lived here for ten years.　10年ずっとここに住んでいる。

「ずっと」という表現に継続のニュアンスを出す。

完了（ちょうど～したところだ，すでに～した）

I have just finished my homework.　ちょうど今宿題が終わったところです。

結果（過去のあるできごとの結果が現在も残っている）

I have lost my room key.　部屋の鍵をなくして持っていません。

I lost my room key. は過去になくしたという事実を述べているだけ。今は見つかって持っているかもしれない。have lost のほうはまだ見つかっていない。

■Help の語法

① help ＋ O（人）with～「O の～を手伝う」

She helps him with his homework.　彼女は彼の宿題を手伝います。

② help（to）do～「～するのを手伝う」

I help（to）wash his car.　私は彼の洗車を手伝う。

③ help ＋ O（人）to do～「O が～するのを手伝う」

I help her（to）make a cake.　私は彼女がケーキをつくるのを手伝う。

■使役動詞

使役とは，他人にある動作を行わせたり，ある事態を引き起こさせたりする意味を表す。大きく以下の3つに分けて考えるとわかりやすい。

① 依頼（～してもらう）

have ＋ O（人）＋ do「O に～してもらう」

I had her get some water.　彼女に水を持ってきてもらった。

I had him wash my car.　私は彼に車を洗ってもらった。

have ＋ O（物）＋ done「O を～してもらう，O が～される」

I had my car washed by him.　彼に車を洗ってもらった。（受益）

I had my wallet stolen yesterday.　昨日財布を盗まれた。（被害）

② 強制（無理やり～される）

make ＋ O（人）＋ do ＝ force ＋ O（人）＋ to do

（O に無理やり～させる）force の代わりに compel も使える。

She made him work all night.　彼女は彼に夜通し勉強させた。

＝She forced him to work all night.

③ 許可（自由に～させる）

let ＋ O（人）＋ do ＝ allow ＋ O（人）＋ to do

（O に自由に～させる）allow の代わりに permit も使える。

She let her kids play on the street.

彼女たちは子どもたちを自由に通りで遊ばせた。

使役動詞を使った文は第5文型 SVOC なので，OC の部分を SV に見立てて考えると理解しやすい。たとえば，

I had him wash my car.
S V O C
↓ ↓
S V

He washed my car.「『彼が私の車を洗う』という状況をもった」と考える。

I had my car washed by him.
↓ ↓
S V

My car was washed by him.「『私の車が彼によって洗われる』という状況をもった」と考える。

theme 2 A Broken Leg

P : Patient　D : Doctor

P : What does the X-ray say?

D : [(1)]

P : [(2)]

D : [(3)]

P : [(4)]

D : Bones need time to heal. We can put it in a cast here and give you crutches. It (a) <u>shouldn't</u> take more than an hour.

P : [(5)]

D : It might take some getting used to, but in order for the bones to mend it's the best thing to do.

P : [(6)]

D : Don't get it wet! Also (b) <u>driving</u> a car would be a little dangerous. The key is to keep your weight on the crutches, not your leg.

設問 上の会話文を読んで次の設問に答えなさい。

1 会話文を完成させるために空所（1）～（6）に適切な英文を（a）～（f）から選んで入れなさい。

(a) A month?!

(b) I've never had a cast before.

(c) What do you recommend?

(d) Are there any restrictions while I have it?

(e) Well, your leg is broken — not too bad, but it's a break. Right here.

(f) We had better put it in a cast — probably for a month.

2 下線部（a）の <u>should</u> の用法と同じ用法の文を次の中から選びなさい。

① You <u>should</u> go out at once.

② You <u>should</u> have done so.

③ We are surprised that you <u>should</u> have said such a thing.

④ According to the weather forecast, it should be raining now.

3 下線部（b）の ～ ing 形の用法と同じ文を次の中から選びなさい。

① She is so busy cleaning her room.

② She went shopping after lunch.

③ What do you say to going out for a walk?

④ It is no use crying over spilt milk.

語句解説

● **say**　～であることを表す，～と書いてある
レントゲン検査（写真）はなにを表していますか → レントゲンの結果はどうでしたか。How does the X-ray look? ともいえる。
This letter says that he quit his job.
彼は仕事を辞めたとこの手紙には書いてある。

● **S is broken.**　Sは壊されている。→ S は壊れている。→ S は骨折です。

● **right here**　ちょうどここ ➡ この right はある位置を指して「ちょうど，すぐ……」の意味で次のように使われる。
right next to him　彼のすぐ隣に／**right in the middle**　ど真ん中

● **cast**　㊔ギブス　㊕～にギブスをはめる ➡ We had better put it in a cast. の it は your broken leg のこと。＝We'll want you to wear a cast.

● **crutch**　松葉杖／**walk on crutches**　松葉杖をついて歩く

● It shouldn't take more than an hour. ➡ should に注意。話し手の確信度を表す助動詞 should で「～だろう，～のはずだ」の意味。

● It might take some getting used to, ……「慣れるのに少し時間がかかるかもしれません」「（時間が）～かかる」の take。この文の it は the cast。
＝It might take some（time）to get used to it, ……ともいえる。

● **get used to～**　～するのに慣れる

● **in order to～**　～するために

● **mend**　治る＝**heal**

● **restrictions**　制限，制約

● **The key is（to）do ～**　大事なことは～することだ
the key to success　成功の鍵

解答はp.19

テーマ 2 足の骨折

患：患者　医：医者

患：レントゲンの結果はどうでしょうか。

医：足の骨が折れています。ひどくはないけど骨折です。ちょうどここのところです。

患：どんな治療をすすめられますか。

医：ギブスをはめたほうがいいでしょう。１か月くらいはかかります。

患：１か月もですか？！

医：骨は治るのに時間がかかります。ここの部分にギブスをはめて松葉杖を使ってもらいます。１時間とかかりません。

患：今までギブスなんてやったことありません。

医：慣れるまでしばらく時間がかかるかもしれませんが，骨が完治するにはこれが１番いい方法です。

患：ギブスをつけているときになにか制約がありますか。

医：濡らさないでください。また車の運転はちょっと危険でしょう。注意してほしいのは，足に体重をかけないで松葉杖にかけるようにすることです。

解答

1 (1) − (e)　(2) − (c)　(3) − (f)　(4) − (a)　(5) − (b)
(6) − (d)

2 ④

3 ④

解説

1 会話の流れから (1) には (e) が，(6) には (d) がくる。(5) にはギブスの不安に対して慣れだという流れから (b)。(2) (3) (4) は (f) (a) の順序が決まれば容易だろう。

2 should　～のはずだ

3 会話文中の driving は動名詞が主語として使われている。
選択肢中の①②は現在分詞とも動名詞とも解釈できる。動名詞だとしたら in～ing の形からきているので，driving の用法とは違う。③の to～ing も同様である。④の It は crying over spilt milk の動名詞句と同じだからこれが正解になる。

① 彼女は部屋の掃除で忙しい。

② 彼女は昼食後買い物に出かけた。

③ 散歩に出かけるのはどうでしょうか。

④ こぼれたミルクを嘆(なげ)いても無駄だ。＝覆水盆(ふくすい)に返らず

文法 語法

■話者の確信度を表す助動詞

could → might → may → can → should → ought to → would → will → must

の順で強くなる。形は過去形でも意味は現在の推量。

could ～の可能性がある，**should** ～のはずだ，**must** ～に違いない

It shouldn't take more than an hour.

ギブスをはめるのに１時間以上はたぶんかからないでしょう。

It might take some getting used to.

ギブスは慣れるまでしばらく時間がかかるでしょう。

Also driving a car would be a little dangerous.

また車の運転はちょっと危険でしょう。

■受身文 be＋過去分詞「～される」

She is liked by everyone in the village.「彼女は村のみんなに好かれている」が基本だが，過去分詞が形容詞化して She is tired. She is disappointed.「疲れている，落胆している」などのように使う場合がある。S is broken.「骨折している」も後者に近いといえる。

■Take「時間が～かかる」の語法

次の２つは構文として覚えておくと便利な表現。

① It takes ＋ (時間) ＋ to do ～「～するのに (時間) がかかる」

It takes five minutes to walk to the station. 駅まで歩いて5分かかる。

② It takes ＋ (人) ＋ (時間) ＋ to do ～「(人) が～するのに (時間) がかかる」

It takes us three days to do the work.

我々がその仕事をするのには3日かかる。

＝It takes three days for us to do the work.

＝The work takes us three days.

＝We take three days to do the work.

＝We take three days doing the work.

■should の語法

① ～のはずだ（当然）

We should arrive before dark.　暗くなる前に着くはずだ。

② ～したほうがいい，～すべきだ（義務，婉曲（えんきょく）な勧め）

You should go at once.　あなたはすぐに出かけたほうがいい。

③ should have ＋過去分詞「～すべきだったのに…」

You should have visited her then.

そのとき彼女を訪ねておけばよかったのに。

④ 感情の should（驚き・残念な気持ちを表す）

I am surprised that he should have done such a foolish thing.

彼がそんな愚かなことをしたなんて驚きだ。

⑤ 提案・要求・必要などを表す that 節中で

We suggested that she should stay there until next month.

彼女は来月まではそこに滞在すべきだと我々は提案した。

➡ アメリカ英語では should stay が stay（原形動詞）となる。stayed や stays とはならないので注意。

■get used to ＋名詞「～するのに慣れる」
be used to ＋名詞「～するのに慣れている」

used の代わりに accustomed も使える。

I'm not used to eating so quickly.　そんな早食いするのは慣れていない。

I'm not used to spicy food.　辛い食べ物には慣れていません。

You will get used to getting up early.　早起きにも慣れてくるでしょう。

■in order to～「～するために」

so as to～もほぼ同じ意味で使える。

ただし in order to は不定詞の意味上の主語をとれる上に文頭にもおける。

In order for us to get there safely we used the jeep.

私たちはそこに無事に着けるようにジープを使った。

They went early so as to be in time for the party.

彼らはパーティーに間に合うように早めに出かけた。

theme 3 A Checkup

D : Doctor　P : Patient

D : [　　　(1)　　　]

P : Nothing special. I just haven't been here for（　2　）a year and thought I ought to have a checkup.

D : How are you feeling?

P : Pretty good. But I've been (3) <u>kind</u> of tired lately.

D : Well, let me listen to your heart and lungs. Are there any changes in your lifestyle? Smoking? Drinking? Diet?

P : No.

D : Hop on the scale.（Later）A few pounds more than last time. What do you do for exercise?

P : I walk [　(4)　] my lunch break almost every day.

D : (5)(good, to, compared, that's, nothing, doing), but something that requires more exertion might be [　(6)　] order. Jogging, or cycling......something that will bring your heart rate up for 20 or 25 minutes.

設問 上の会話文を読んで次の設問に答えなさい。

1 空所（1）には医者が「どうしましたか」という意味の文が入る。次の中から選びなさい。

(A) Like what?　(B) What's the problem?

(C) What are you doing?　(D) What do you do?　(E) What for?

2 空所（2）には「～以上」という意味の単語が入る。次の中から選びなさい。

(A) over　(B) through　(C) up　(D) beyond　(E) on

3 下線部（3）の kind と同じ用法で使われている文を１つ選びなさい。

(A) She's so kind that everybody loves her.

(B) It's very kind of you to show me the way to the station.

(C) She is my kind of girl.

(D) She seemed kind of depressed.

4 空所（4）には「〜中」「〜の間」の意味の単語が入る。次から選びなさい。

(A) in　(B) while　(C) among　(D) during

5 （5）のカッコ内の単語を「なにもしないよりいいことです」という意味になるように並べ替えなさい。

6 空所（6）に入る適当な語句を次の中から選びなさい。

(A) in　(B) of　(C) at　(D) on　(E) out of

語句解説

- **checkup**　健康診断＝**physical checkup**＝**medical checkup**
- **What's the problem?**　問題はなんですか。→どうしましたか。➡ 医者がよく使う決まり文句＝**What's the matter?**
- **for over a year**　1年以上もの間
- **ought to**＝**should**　〜すべきである（義務・婉曲(えんきょく)な命令）
- **feel good**　気分がいい／**feel well**（身体の）調子がいい
- kind of ➡ 表現を弱めるために口語ではよく使い「いくぶん，少し」の意味。kinada, kinder のように表記することもある。似た表現に sort of がある。
- **lately**＝**recently**　最近
- **let me do〜**　〜させてください→〜してみましょう
- **hop on**＝**get on**　〜に（飛び）乗る／**hop on a train**　電車に飛び乗る
- **lunch break**　昼休み ➡ この break は休み，休憩の意味。
  coffee break　コーヒーブレイク
- Compared to doing nothing, that's good. ➡ 分詞構文の文。接続詞を補って考えると，If walking is compared to doing nothing, that's good.「もし歩くのがなにもしないのと比較されれば，それはいいことです」が直訳。
  compare A with B　AとBを比較する ➡ with が to になる場合がある。
  compare A to B　AをBにたとえる
- **exertion**　激しい運動
- **be in order**　〜にふさわしい，〜に適切だ。⇔ **be out of order**　故障している，不具合だ。

解答はp.25

テーマ 3 健康診断

医：医者　患：患者

医：どうしましたか。

患：いえとくに。１年ぶりなので健康診断を受けたほうがいいと思って。

医：気分はいいですか。

患：いいです。最近少し疲れぎみですけど……

医：聴診器をあててみましょう。なにか生活スタイルに変化はありますか。たとえばタバコ，飲酒，ダイエットなど。

患：いいえ，ありません。

医：では体重計に乗ってみてください。（しばらくして）前回より数ポンド増えています。なにか運動をしていますか。

患：昼休みに歩いています。ほとんど毎日。

医：なにもしないよりいいことですが，もっとなにか運動量の多いものがいいでしょう。ジョギングかサイクリング……心拍数が上がるようななにか運動を20分か25分ほど。

解答

1 (B)

2 (A)

3 (D)

4 (D)

5 Compared to doing nothing, that's good

6 (A)

解説

1 (A) たとえば，どんな？
(B) どうしましたか？
(C) なにをしているんですか？
(D) なにをしていらっしゃるんですか？（職業を訊く）
(E) なんのため？／なぜ？

2 「～以上」over = more than

3 kind of tired lately. の kind of は「少し，ちょっと」といった意味。会話ではよく使われる。
(A) 彼女はとても優しいのでみんな彼女のことが好きだ。(so～that…)
(B) 来てくださってご親切にどうもありがとう。(It is～of + O + to do….)
(C) 彼女は私の好きなタイプの女の子だ。
(D) 彼女はちょっと落ち込んでいるように見えた。

4 during と while の違いはよく出題される。両方とも「～の間」という意味だが，while は接続詞で，during は前置詞。
During my stay in Paris ＝While I was staying in Paris

5 分詞構文の部分，Compared to doing nothing ができるかがポイント。
Compared with（to）the body, her hands seemed oversized.
彼女の身体から比較して手は際立って大きく見えた。
接続詞を補えば次のようになる。
If her hands were compared to the body, her hands seemed oversized.

6 In order ～にふさわしい，～に適切だ

文法 語法

■分詞構文＝現在分詞，過去分詞を副詞的に使った表現形式

① When he saw her, he ran way.

→ Seeing her, he ran away.　彼は彼女を見かけると逃げた。

② Since he was terrified of being scolded, he told a lie.

→ Terrified of being scolded, he told a lie.
怒られることを恐れて彼はうそをついた。

③ The train leaves Tokyo at seven and arrives in Osaka at ten.

→ The train leaves Tokyo at seven, arriving in Osaka at ten.
その電車は東京を7時に出て10時に大阪に着く。

④ As I didn't know what to do, I asked Tom for help.

→ Not knowing what to do, I asked Tom for help.
どうしていいかわからなかったので，私はトムに助けを求めた。

⑤ Though he has failed several times, he still hopes for success.

→ Having failed several times, he still hopes for success.
彼は何度も失敗したけれども成功をまだ望んでいる。

■During／While「～の間に」の語法

During my stay in Paris, I met her.
＝While I was staying in Paris, I met her.
パリにいるときに私は彼女に会いました。

■In spite of／despite／though／although「～にもかかわらず」の語法

In spite of her age, she still leads an active life.
＝Despite her age, she still leads an active life.
＝Though（Although）she is old, she still leads an active life.
彼女は高齢にもかかわらず，いまだに活動的な生活を送っている。

痛みの表現方法①

◇ache

I ache all over. = My body aches all over.　全身が痛みます。

My arms ache.　腕が痛みます。

I have a headache.　頭が痛い。／頭痛がする。

My eyes ache from want of sleep.　睡眠不足から目が痛い。

I have an ache in my side.　脇腹が痛む。

◇hurt

It hurts.　痛いです。

My elbow hurts when I bend it.　ひじを曲げると痛みます。

He hurt his leg when he fell.　彼は転んだとき足を痛めた。

My tooth hurts when I eat anything cold. = Cold food makes my tooth hurt.　冷たい食べものを食べると歯にしみる。

My son fell off a swing and hurt his head.

息子がブランコから落ちて頭にけがをしました。

◇pain

I had a terrible pain in my back.　背中にズキズキする痛みを感じた。

I feel a great deal of pain in my head.　ひどい頭痛がする。

I feel sharp pain in my lower back.　腰に激しい痛みを感じます。

I have a severe pain in the back and it is killing me.

背中に激痛がして死にそうだ。

acheは継続的な鋭い痛み，hurtは打ち身や傷による痛み，painは急な不快な痛みを表す。

theme 4 Chicken Pox

M : Mother　N : Nurse

(Mother calls the doctor's office)

M : Hello, my daughter needs to see the doctor.

N : What's the matter, Mrs. ......?

M : Silk. Jane Silk. My daughter, Jane, is one of Dr. Borah's patients. (1) She has spots all over her body.

N : How old is she?

M : She'll be four next month.

N : Do they itch?

M : Yes! (2) She's scratching them all the time.

N : Does she have a fever?

M : A slight one. At night.

N : Sounds (3) like chicken pox. But you'd better bring her in (4) so we can take a look at her.

設問 上の会話文を読んで次の設問に答えなさい。

1 下線部（1）（2）を日本語に訳しなさい。

2 下線部（3）と同じ用法の like を次の中から選びなさい。1つとは限らない。

(A) They like chicken very much.

(B) What's your boyfriend like?

(C) Don't look at me like that.

(D) I'll do it like you do.

3 下線部（4）と同じ用法の so を次の中から選びなさい。

(A) He became very poor, so he sold up his luxurious imported cars.

(B) Jane speaks English very well and so does her sister.

(C) It is hot today. So it is.

(D) She took a taxi so that she would be in time for the party.

語句解説

- **see** （医者に）診てもらう
- **What's the matter?** （娘さん）どうしましたか。➡ この the matter は「困ったこと，支障，故障」の意味。
  Something is the matter with this radio. = Something is wrong with this radio.
  = There is something wrong with this radio.
- **spot** 斑点（はんてん），ぶつぶつ
- **all over** 〜中／**all over the world** 世界中
- **itch** 動 〜がかゆい
- She's scratching them all the time. ➡ them は the spots のこと。
  all the time「いつも」,「身体中をひっかいてばかりいる」なら She's scratching them all over her body. となる。
  ➡ 現在進行形で「いつも〜してばかりいる」という不平不満の表現になっている。
  He's watching TV on the couch. 彼は長いすでテレビばかり見ている。
- **fever** 熱
  Any fever? = Does she have a fever? 彼女は熱がありますか。
- a slight one の one は fever のこと。
- **sound like〜** 〜のように聞こえる
  (That) sounds good. それはいいですね。／**That sounds like an interesting idea.** それは面白そうな考えに思われます。→ それは面白そうですね。
- **had better** 〜したほうがいい
  I had better see a doctor. 私は医者に診てもらったほうがよさそうだ。
- **bring + 人 + in** 「人 を連れて来る」in のあとに our office が省略されている。
  この反対は **take + 人 + to** 場所 「人 を〜に連れて行く」。
- **〜so…** …するために〜，〜そうすれば…（so that…の that の省略）
- **take a look at〜 = look at** 〜をひと目見る，ちょっと見る

解答はp.31

テーマ 4 水疱瘡（みずぼうそう）

母：母親　看：看護師

（母親が病院に電話します）

母：こんにちは。娘が先生に診てもらいたいのですが……

看：どうしました。お名前をお願いします。

母：シルク。ジェーン・シルクです。娘のジェーンのかかりつけの医者はボラ先生です。身体中に斑点ができているんです。

看：何歳ですか。

母：来月4歳になります。

看：かゆがっていますか。

母：はい。ひっかいてばかりいます。

看：熱はどうですか。

母：少しあります。夜に。

看：みずぼうそうのようですね。連れて来てみてください。診てみますから。

解答

1 (1) 彼女は身体中にぶつぶつができました。

(2) 彼女はいつもひっかいてばかりいます。

2 (B)(C)

3 (D)

解説

1 (1) **spots** 斑点，ぶつぶつ ➡ all over「～中」が訳出のポイント。

(2) 現在進行形を「いつも～してばかりいる」，all the time＝always が訳せるかがポイント。

2 Sounds like chicken pox. の like は「～のように」の意味の前置詞，look like「～のように見える」，feel like「～のように感じる」，smell like「～のようなにおいがする」，taste like「～のような味がする」のように使う。

(A) 彼らは鶏肉がとても好きだ。

(B) 君のボーイフレンドはどんな人？

(C) そんなふうに私を見ないで。

(D) 君がするように僕もやってみよう。（接続詞で like を使った例）

3 ～so that…「…するために（目的）」の that が省略された形。

(A) 彼は貧乏になったので自分のもっていた高級外車を売った。

(B) ジェーンは英語を流暢（りゅうちょう）に話すが彼女の妹もそうだ。

(C) 今日は暑い！！　本当にそうですね。

(D) 彼女はパーティーに間に合うようにタクシーに乗った。

文法 語法

■so（that）の用法

① I have no money right now, so I have no lunch today.
今お金がないので今日は昼抜きです。**「～だから（それゆえ）…」**（結果）

② Come home early so we can have dinner together.
一緒に夕食が食べられるように早く帰ってきてね。**「…するために～」**（目的）
「彼は成功するために懸命に働いた」は次のようにいえる。

He worked hard so that he might succeed.
He worked hard so he might succeed.
He worked hard that he might succeed.
He worked hard in order that he might succeed.
He worked hard in order to succeed.
He worked hard so as to succeed.

■have ＋ a ＋名詞

have（get, take）a look at ～をひと目見る，**have（take）a walk** 散歩する，**have a talk** 話をする，**have a good time** 楽しむ，**have a drink** 1杯のむ，**have a bite** 軽く食べる，**have an argument** 議論する，**have a try** やってみる

■現在進行形の用法

① 進行中の動作
I'm doing my homework now. 今，宿題をしているところです。

② 不平・不満
You're always complaining about your work.
君はいつも仕事の不満ばかり言ってるね。

③ 確定的な未来・予定
He is flying to New York tomorrow morning.
彼は明日の朝飛行機でニューヨークに向かいます。

■勧めの表現（had betterなど）

① had better～したほうがいい（そうでないと困ったことになる）［警告的勧め］

You had better see a doctor at once.

すぐに医者に診てもらわないと（大変なことになるよ）。

意味的に強いので I（一人称）か目下に対して使うほうが無難。口語では had が省略されて（You）better leave now.（もう出発したほうがいい）のように使う。

② should「～したほうがいい，～すべきだ」［義務・必要］**＝ought to**

You should see a doctor.　医者に診てもらうべきだよ。

③ may（might）as well「～したほうがしないよりいいのでは…」［消極的勧め］

You may as well see a doctor.　医者に診てもらったほうがいいのでは…。

強さ的には，may as well < should < ought to < had better

■sound like「～のように聞こえる」の like の語法

この like は前置詞で look, feel, seem, be などの動詞と一緒に使える。

Your forehead is like your father's.　君のおでこはお父さんにそっくりだ。

When the house is painted, it will look like new.

ペンキを塗ったら家は新築のように見えるでしょう。

I feel like（having）a beer.　ビールを一杯といきたい感じだ。

like には他に接続詞としての用法がある。

Please do it like I tell you.　私が言うようにやってください。

It looks like we're going to have a heavy rain.　大雨になりそうだ。

theme 5 Insomnia

D : Doctor　P : Patient

D : So you're having trouble [(1)]?

P : Yeah. I get [(2)] okay, but then I wake up a few hours later and can't get back [(3)].

D : When did you first [(4)] this?

P : Almost a month ago. I'm [(5)] all day.

D : Are there any big [(6)] in your life? Work? Family?

P : Work is okay. Our new computer system is [(7)], but everyone feels [(8)]. We're going to have baby in November, but I'm happy [(9)].

D : Still, a baby and work, that's a lot to think about. Tell me about your [(10)], and how much [(11)] you drink.

P : I jog fifty minutes on Sunday and I drink two cups of coffee a day.

D : When do you drink coffee?

設問 上の会話文を完成するために（1）～（11）の空所に入れるのに最も適当な語を次の（A）～（M）から１つずつ選びなさい。ただし同じものを２回使う所がある。

(A) about that	(B) a nightmare	(C) tired	(D) that way
(E) sleep	(F) sleeping	(G) to sleep	(H) slept
(I) exercise	(J) coffee or tea	(K) notice	(L) changes
(M) well			

語句解説

- **insomnia**　不眠症
- **have trouble（in）～ing**　～するのに苦労する

  The student had trouble finding work after graduation.

  その学生は卒業後なかなか仕事が見つからず困った。
- **get to sleep okay**　よく寝つける
- **wake up**　目覚める
- **get back to sleep**　眠りに戻る
- **When did you first notice this?**

  このことにいつ初めて気づきましたか。→いつからですか。
- **nightmare**　悪夢
- **We are going to have a baby.＝We are gonna have a baby.**

  赤ちゃんが生まれるんです。

  ➡ be going to「～するつもりです，～することになる」（確定した予定）は会話では be gonna で使われる。
- **still**（接続詞的に用いて）それでもなお，それでも（＝**but still**）
- Tell me about your exercise, and how much coffee or tea you drink.

  ➡ Tell me about のあとに exercise と how much coffee or tea you drink の 2 つの目的語が続いている。

解答はp.37

テーマ 5 不眠症

医：医者　患：患者

医：眠れなくて困っているんですね。

患：はい。よく寝つけるんですが，数時間後に目が覚めてそれからあと眠れないんです。

医：いつからですか。

患：１か月前からです。１日中疲れた状態です。

医：生活になにか大きな変化がありましたか。仕事とか家庭で…

患：仕事は大丈夫です。新しく導入したコンピューターシステムは悪夢のようなものですが，社内のみんながそんな風に感じています。11月に赤ちゃんが生まれる予定なんですが，それはハッピーなことだし……

医：それでも，赤ちゃんや仕事に関しては考えることがたくさんありますね。ところで，運動とカフェインをどのくらいとっているか教えてもらえますか。

患：日曜日に50分ほどジョギングをします。コーヒーを１日に２杯飲みます。

医：コーヒーはいつ飲んでますか。

解答

(1) − (F)　(2) − (G)　(3) − (G)　(4) − (K)
(5) − (C)　(6) − (L)　(7) − (B)　(8) − (D)
(9) − (A)　(10) − (I)　(11) − (J)

解説

have trouble〜ing から（1）は（F）と決まる。次に get to＝〜を始める，get back to＝〜に戻る，から（2）（3）に（G）がくる。（4）は動詞の原形が入るが意味から（K）しかない。（8）が難しいが **that way** で「そのように」の意味で feel のあとがつながる。他は文脈から単語の意味さえわかれば容易だろう。

知っておきたいことわざ①

□病は気から

The mind rules the body.

□腹八分に医者いらず

Temperance is the best physic.

文法語法

■trouble／spend／busy の構文

① **have trouble（in）～ing「～するのに苦労する」＝have difficulty～ing**

I had a lot of difficulty getting this CD.

私はこのCDを手に入れるのにたいへん苦労した。

② **spend ＋ O ＋（in）～ing「～するのに O を使う」**

I spent a week doing nothing there.

私はそこでなにもしないで１週間過ごした。

③ **be busy（in）～ing「～で忙しい」**

I'm busy taking care of my baby.　赤ちゃんの世話で忙しくしています。

■Tell の語法

① **tell ＋ O_1 ＋ O_2**

She told her children a story. = She told a story to her children.

彼女は子ども達に話をしてあげた。

He told me that he would have a try.　彼は私にもう１回やってみると言った。

Tell me how old she is.　彼女が何歳か教えてください。

② **tell ＋ O ＋ about～「O に～について話す」**

I told her about the accident.　私は彼女にその事故について話した。

③ **tell ＋ O ＋ to do「O に～するようにいう」**

He told me to go out instead of staying at home.

彼は私に家にいないで外出するように言った。

④ **tell ＋ O_1 ＋ from ＋ O_2「O_1 と O_2 を区別する」**

Can you tell Jane from her sister?

ジェーンと彼女のお姉さんを見分けられますか。

■be going to の語法

① **確定した予定**

We are going to leave Japan for Switzerland in July.

私たちは7月にスイスに向けて日本を発ちます。

（ビザや航空券の手配がすんでいて確定した予定になっている）

② 現在の兆候などに基づく未来予測

It's going to rain.　雨になりそうだ。

③ 主語の意図・確信

I'm going to be a pilot. = I will be a pilot.　パイロットになるつもりだ。

■SVO$_1$ + O$_2$ で O$_1$ + O$_2$ の入れ換え

第 4 文型の文で間接目的語 O$_1$ を直接目的語 O$_2$ のあとにもってくると，前置詞に to を用いる動詞と for を用いる動詞，その他の前置詞を用いる動詞に分けられる。

① to をとる動詞

She gave me an English book.　彼女は私に英語の本をくれた。（SVO$_1$O$_2$）

She gave an English book to me.　彼女は私に英語の本をくれた。（SVO − 第3文型）

give 以外に write, read, lend, bring, sell, send, teach, tell, pay などがある。

② for をとる動詞

He bought his daughter a doll.　彼は娘に人形を買ってあげた。（SVO$_1$O$_2$）

He bought a doll for his daughter.　彼は娘に人形を買ってあげた。（SVO = 第3文型）

buy 以外に make, get, cook, do, find, choose などがある。

③ その他の前置詞

次のような動詞に限定される。

They played him a trick.　彼らは彼にいたずらをした。

→ They played a trick on him.

He asked her a favor.　彼は彼女に頼みごとをした。

→ He asked a favor of her.

theme 6 An Allergy

P : Patient　D : Doctor

P : I think I have a cold. I'm [(1)] a lot and my eyes are itchy.

D : Are you coughing?

P : No. I'm just [(2)] my nose a lot.

D : Do you have any allergies?

P : I don't know. Why?

D : It's spring. A lot of people are allergic [(3)] grass or flower pollen, especially in the country. Try DRISTAN — you don't need a prescription [(4)] it. If it doesn't work, let us know. We can [(5)] something stronger.

P : Are allergies like this serious?

D : Not usually. They're pretty similar [(6)] colds, and some people get them every year at this time.

P : But this is the first spring I've ever felt this way.

D : Where did you live before [(7)] here?

P : Chicago.

D : Right [(8)] the middle of the city.

P : Yes, downtown.

D : That [(9)] it. In big cities, there usually isn't enough grass or whatever to make it a problem for you. But the first time you're in the country, it really [(10)] you.

設問 上の会話文を読んで次の設問に答えなさい。

1 空所（1）（2）（5）（7）（9）（10）に入る適語を次の中から１つずつ選びなさい。

(A) prescribe　(B) explains　(C) blowing

(D) hits　(E) sneezing　(F) moving

2 空所（3）（4）（6）（8）に入る前置詞を次の中から１つずつ選びなさい。

(A) in　(B) on　(C) at　(D) to

(E) of　(F) from　(G) for　(H) over

語句解説

- **allergy**　アレルギー　形 **allergic**　アレルギーの

  I'm allergic to natto.　私は納豆が苦手なんです。
- **have a cold**　風邪をひいている／**catch a cold**　風邪をひく
- **sneeze**　くしゃみをする

  I'm sneezing a lot.　くしゃみをしてばっかりいるんです。
- **itch**　～がかゆい
- **blow one's nose**　鼻をかむ
- **A lot of people are allergic to grass or flowers.**

  多くの人たちが草や花に対してアレルギーを起こす。

  be allergic to～　～に対してアレルギーを起こす
- **especially in the country**　とくに田舎（いなか）では
- **DRISTAN**　ドリスタン ➡ 花粉症（hay fever）に効く市販薬。
- **prescription**　処方箋（せん）
- **work**　動（薬などが）効く
- **serious**（病気などが）重い，深刻な
- **not usually**　いつも～というわけではない → そうでもないですよ
- **be similar to～**　～に似ている ➡ ここの文で使われている pretty は similar を修飾する副詞で「とても，かなり」の意味。
- **right in the middle of～**　～のちょうど真ん中 ➡ right は強調の副詞，たとえば **right then**　ちょうどそのとき，**right before breakfast**　朝食の直前に。
- **downtown**　中心街，繁華街／**go downtown**　町へ買い物などに出かける
- That explains it. ➡「ここに引っ越してくる前にシカゴの中心街に住んでいたことが，この春から花粉症になったことを説明している」が直訳。
- **it really hits you.**　田舎の草木や花の花粉があなたを直撃する。➡ この文の hits は「～を直撃する，～に打撃を与える」。

解答はp.43

テーマ 6 アレルギー

患：患者　医：医者

患：風邪をひいたみたいです。くしゃみがよく出て，目がかゆいんです。
医：咳はどうですか。
患：咳は出ません。鼻をかんでばかりいるんです。
医：なにかアレルギーはありますか。
患：わかりません。どうしてですか。
医：春ですから，多くの人たちが花粉症になっています。とくに田舎のほうでは。ドリスタンを服用してみてください。処方箋はいりませんから。効かないときは知らせてください。もっと強い薬を処方しますから。
患：このようなアレルギーは重いものですか。
医：そうでもないですよ。風邪にとてもよく似ていて一部の人はこの時期になると毎年かかります。
患：でもこのようになったのはこの春が初めてなんです。
医：ここに引っ越す前はどこに住んでいましたか。
患：シカゴです。
医：市の中心部ですか。
患：はい，繁華街です。
医：それでわかりました。大都市には問題になるような草花があまりありません。しかし田舎に引っ越した当初はそれが大変な悩みになるんです。

解答

1 (1) − (E)　(2) − (C)　(5) − (A)　(7) − (F)　(9) − (B)
(10) − (D)

2 (3) − (D)　(4) − (G)　(6) − (D)　(8) − (A)

解説

1 (1) は症状を訴えている場面だから (E) と決まる。(2) は blow one's nose からすぐ (C) とわかるはず。(5) は can のあとだから原形動詞の (A) が確定。(7) は before のあとなので動名詞を選ぶので (F) しかない。(9)(10) は文脈と That explains it.「それでわかりました」が思いつけばすべて決まる。

2 (3) は be allergic to　～に対してアレルギーを起こす

(4) ～に対する処方箋となるから for

(6) be similar to　～に似ている

(8) in the middle of　～の真ん中

知っておきたいことわざ②

□風邪は万病のもと

A cold may develop into all kinds of illness.

□笑いにまさる薬はなし

Laughter is the best medicine.

文法 語法

■使役動詞 let　let＋㊇＋do「㊇に自由に～させる」

I let my child play in the sandbox.　子どもを自由に砂場で遊ばせた。

Let me explain how to do the work.　仕事のやりかたを説明しましょう。

■make＋O＋C「OをCにする」

I made her happy.　私は彼女を幸せにした。

I made her my secretary.　私は彼女を自分の秘書にしました。

I made her disappointed.　私は彼女をがっかりさせました。

She made him study all night.　彼女は彼を一晩中勉強させた。

Cには形容詞，名詞，過去分詞，原形不定詞などが用いられる。

■部分否定　not usually「いつも～ではない」

She doesn't usually eat lunch.　彼女はいつも昼食を食べるわけではない。

➡ ただし She usually doesn't eat lunch. は，彼女は普通昼食は食べない，となる。

Not all children like apples.　すべての子どもがりんごを好きとは限らない。

I haven't read both books.　両方の本を読んだわけではない。

I'm not always free on Sundays.　日曜日がいつも暇（ひま）とは限らない。

痛みの表現方法②

◇その他

Ouch!　痛い／熱い

My eyes feel irritated.　目がチカチカする。

I have sore shoulders.　肩が痛い（過度の運動で）。

I have stiff shoulders. = My shoulders are stiff.　肩がこって痛い。

My legs itch. = My legs are itching.　足がむずがゆい。

My back is killing me.　背中が死ぬほど痛い。

I am having severe cramps.　ひどい生理痛です。

I have a problem with heartburn.　胸やけがする。

患者の使う決まり文句（症状の表現）①

I have a fever.　熱があります。

I have a high temperature.　高熱があります。

I have a fever of 102 degrees.　102度の高熱です。

I've been sick for the last couple of days.　ここ2〜3日具合が悪いんです。

I feel a chill.　悪寒がします。

I feel feverish.　熱っぽいです。

I have a cold.　風邪をひいています。

I have a sore throat.　のどが痛い。

I think I may have a cold.　風邪をひいたようです。

I have had a cough.　咳が続いています。

I have been having severe headaches for the past two days.

この2日間ひどい頭痛なのです。

I have very high blood pressure.　血圧がとても高いのです。

I have no appetite.　食欲がありません。

theme 7 A Urine Test

N : Nurse　M : Bobby's mother　B : Bobby

N : How is Bobby today?

M : Pretty good. [(1)] but he's pretty busy at school.

N : Good. We'll need a urine sample today. Bobby, can you go to the bathroom for us?

B : But I don't have to go.

N : Well, [(2)] and try for us, okay?

M : Come on, Bobby! Drink some water.

N : [(3)], I'll take it when you're done.

M : Exactly [(4)]?

N : [(5)], such as blood, which could signal an infection, and we'll check the sugar level for diabetes.

設問 上の会話文の空所（1）～（5）に以下の日本語の意味になるよう単語を並び替えて正しい英文にしなさい。

(1) 彼はとても疲れたように見えます
(tired, a, he, seems, lot)

(2) 水をコップ1杯飲んでみたらどうかしら
(have, about, if, how, water, a, you, glass, of)

(3) もし彼をうまく説得して尿をこの容器にとれたら
(this, you, him, go, jar, in, if, can, have)

(4) なんのために彼の尿を検査するんですか
(you, urine, for, test, what, will, his)

(5) 私たちはいろいろなことが調べられます
(things, a, look, will, number, we, of, for)

語句解説

- **I don't have to go（to the bathroom）. = I don't feel like going.**
  私は手洗いに行く必要はありません。→ 今出ないんだ。
  the bathroom = the toilet
- **…, how about if～　and…?**
  水をコップ 1 杯飲んで頑張ってみてくれないかしら。
- **Come on!**　さあ早く（せかすときの表現）
- If you can have him go in this jar,……
  ➡ 使役動詞 have は have + ㊇ + do の形で使う。「㊇ に～させる」，have の代わりに make も使える。
  go は「うまくいく・成功する」の意味。
- **I'll take it when you're done. = I'll take his urine when you're finished.**
  彼の尿をうまくとれたら，それを取りにきます。
- **exactly**　正確に
- **What～for?**　～はなんのためですか。（理由を尋ねる表現）➡ what は for の目的語。What for? という形でも使える。
- **look for～**　～をさがす
- **a number of = many**　たくさんの／**the number of**　～の数
- **～, such as……**　～たとえば……，……のような～
- **infection**　感染，伝染病
- **diabetes**　糖尿病

解答はp.49

テーマ 7 尿検査

看：看護師　母：ボビーの母親　ボ：ボビー

看：ボビーは今日は具合はどうですか。
母：とてもいいですよ。とても疲れて見えますが学校がとても忙しいんです。
看：それはいいですね。今日は採尿します。ボビー手洗いに行ってきてくれる。
ボ：今おしっこしたくないんだもん。
看：じゃ水をコップで１杯飲んで頑張ってみてよ，いい？
母：さあ，ボビー。お水を飲みましょうね。
看：この容器に尿がとれたら取りにきます。
母：なんのために尿検査をするんですか。
看：いろいろなことがわかります。たとえば血液 ── これは病菌に冒(おか)されているかがわかります。また，小児糖尿病かどうかの血糖値も調べます。

解答

（1）He seems tired a lot

（2）how about if you have a glass of water

（3）If you can have him go in this jar

（4）what will you test his urine for

（5）We will look for a number of things

解説

(1) seem＋C から seems tired がつくれれば，あとは容易。

(2) How about～? に if 節が続く形をつくる。

(3) have＋㊇＋do がわかれば，あとはつくれるはず。

(4) What～for?「なんのため，なぜ」を見抜く。

(5) look for～「～をさがす」，a number of～「多くの～」を見抜ければ楽。

知っておきたいことわざ③

□医者の不養生

It is a good physician that follows his own advice.

A physician breaks the rules of health.

He is a good doctor who cures himself.

Doctors often neglect their own health.

文法 語法

■How about～?／What about～?「～はどうですか」

➡ 提案・勧誘・意見を求める表現

How about（going on）a picnic?　ピクニックに行きませんか。

How about another cup of coffee?　もう１杯コーヒーいかがですか。

How about your travel?　旅行どうでしたか。

■What～for?「～はなんのためですか」「なぜ～」

What is the yellow ribbon for?　その黄色のリボンはなんのためですか。

What did you read the book for?　なぜその本を読んだんですか。

＝Why did you read the book?

What～like?「～はどんなですか」も一緒に覚えておこう。

What is she like?　彼女はどんな人ですか。← She is like what?

■a number of＝many「たくさんの」

A number of passengers were injured in the traffic accident.

多くの乗客がその交通事故で負傷した。

➡ a great number of～のように number の前に great, good, large などをつけて「(かなり) 多くの～」と強調する場合もある。

■A such as B＝such A as B「B のような A」

Children want to see animals such as elephants.＝Children want to see such animals as elephants.　子どもたちは象のような動物を見たがっている。

We have a large number of animals, such as elephants, tigers, lions and giraffes.

我々は象，虎，ライオン，キリンのような多くの動物を飼っている。

I've been to several countries of Southeast Asia, such as Thailand, Vietnam and Singapore.　私はタイ，ベトナム，シンガポールといった東南アジアの国々を訪れたことがある。

患者の使う決まり文句（症状の表現）②

I have a stomachache.　お腹が痛い。

I have a sharp pain in my stomach.　胃がキリキリ痛みます。

I have a stuffy nose.　鼻がつまっています。

I have a runny nose.　鼻水が出ます。

I have difficulty breathing.　息が苦しい。

I'm a little short of breath.　ちょっと息切れがします。

I have loose bowels.　お腹がゆるい。

I have diarrhea. = I've got the runs.　下痢をしています。

I feel dizzy.　めまいがします。

I have a terrible pain in my ear.　耳がとても痛い。

I have a toothache.　歯が痛い。

My gums bleed very easily.　歯茎からすぐ血が出ます。

My filling fell out.　詰めてあるのがとれました。

My wisdom tooth is killing me.　親知らずがものすごく痛みます。

My eyes keep watering excessively.　涙が出すぎる。

My right eye itches so much that I keep rubbing it.

右目がかゆくてこすってばかりいます。

I've got ringing in my ears. = My ears are ringing.　耳鳴りがする。

I have been having dizzy spells.　最近めまいがします。

I have blood in my urine.　血尿が出ます。

I noticed bleeding when I urinate.　排尿のときに出血に気づきました。

I have pain when urinating.　排尿時に痛みがある。

I hurt my ankle playing soccer.　サッカーで足首を痛めました。

I cut my finger, and it has become infected.

指を切ってそこが化膿してきました。

I have pain in here.　ここが痛いんです。

theme 8 A Check for Cancer

J : Mrs. Johnson　D : Doctor

J : Frankly, I'm a little concerned. [(1)].

D : [(2)]. Nurse, please come over here.

[(3)]

J : Here.（Doctor examines her）

D : Hmmm. [(4)]. Nothing then.

[(5)].

J : Should I be worried?

D : [(6)]. Tell me about your family. Is there any breast cancer in your family history?

J : [(7)], but I think my grandmother had a breast removed. Is that important?

D : Yes, it can be. [(8)].

設問 上の会話文中の空所（1）～（8）に入れるのに適当な文を下の（A）～（H）からそれぞれ１つずつ選び対話を完成させなさい。

(A) Can you show us where?

(B) Your last mammogram was two years ago

(C) My mother hasn't had any problems

(D) I was doing a self exam this Monday and felt what I think was a lump

(E) We'll know more after the mammogram

(F) You're wise to do self exams

(G) It tends to run in families, but skip generations

(H) We should do another one now to get a better idea

語句解説

- **cancer**　がん
- **frankly**　率直に言って／**frankly speaking**　とも言える
- **I'm a little concerned.**　少し心配しています。➡ **concern**＝**worry**（人を）心配させる

  Her illness concerns her parents.

  ＝**Her parents are concerned about her illness.**

  彼女の両親は彼女の病気のことを心配している。
- **and felt what I think was a lump**　しこりではないかと思うものに触れた

  ➡ **feel**　～に触れる，**lump**　しこり，what は先行詞を含む主格の関係代名詞。

  what is right　正しいこと → **what I think is right**　私が正しいと思うこと

  what he says　彼の言うこと／**what he is**　現在の彼／**what he was**　昔の彼
- **Can you show me where（the lump is）?**

  そのしこりがどこにあるか教えてくれますか。
- **mammogram**　乳房X線写真／**mammography**　乳房X線撮影（法）
- **We should do another one now……**

  私たちは今一度X線検査をするべきです。

  one＝mammogram ➡ We を使うことで You より表現が婉曲（えんきょく）になる。
- **Should I be worried?**　私は心配すべきですか。→ 心配するほどのものでしょうか。
- **Is there any breast cancer in your family history?**

  あなたの家系には乳がんの血統がありますか。→ 家系（家族）に乳がんの人がいますか。Is there any family history of breast cancer?＝Is there any history of breast cancer in your family?＝Does breast cancer run in your family?ともいえる。
- **my grandmother had a breast removed**　祖母は乳房を切除された → 祖母は（乳がんで）乳房を切除した

  had は使役動詞 → have＋O＋過去分詞

  I had my TV fixed at that store.　その店でテレビを修理してもらった。

  I had my wallet stolen on the train.　電車の中で財布を盗まれた。
- **Yes, it can be（important）.**　それは大事なこともあります。

  ➡ 可能性のcan（～のこともある）。

解答はp.55

テーマ 8 がん検査

ジ：ジョンソン婦人　医：医者

ジ：実は，月曜日に自分で胸を触診しましたら，しこりではないかと思うものがあったのでちょっと心配しているんです。

医：ご自分で調べてみられるとはえらいですね。看護師さん，ちょっとこちらへ。どこか教えてくれますか。

ジ：ここです。(医者が触診します)

医：うむ～。最後の乳がんのＸ線検査は２年前でしたね。そのときはなにも異常ありませんでした。どうしたらいいかもう１度Ｘ線検査をやってみましょう。

ジ：心配しなければなりませんか。

医：Ｘ線検査のあとにもっとよくわかるでしょう。家族について教えてください。家系に乳がんの人がいますか。

ジ：母親はなにも問題はありませんが，祖母ががんで乳房をとったと思います。大事なことですか。

医：そういうこともあります。がんは遺伝する傾向があって隔世遺伝もします。

解答

(1) − (D)　(2) − (F)　(3) − (A)　(4) − (B)　(5) − (H)
(6) − (E)　(7) − (C)　(8) − (G)

解説

選択肢の中で self exam に注目すると，(D) (F) の順で (1) (2) に入る。(3) は Here から (A) がくる。次に，Nothing then.「そのときはなにも異常ありませんでした」から mammogram のことだとわかれば，(4) (5) (6) に (B) (H) (E) がくる。(7) は文脈から乳がんの家系かどうか尋ねているので (C) が入り，最後が残りの (G) で確定する。

知っておきたいことわざ④

□習うより慣れよ
Practice makes perfect.
□今日の一針，明日の十針
A stitch in time saves nine.

文法 語法

■関係代名詞

代名詞のはたらきと接続詞のはたらきを兼ねる語で，名詞を修飾する。

基本 I have a friend. **He** lives in New York.

→ I have a friend who lives in New York.

私にはニューヨークに住んでいる友達がいる。

Please show me the coin. You have **it** in your hand.

→ Please show me the coin which you have in your hand.

手の中に持っているコインを私に見せてください。

Please show me **what** you have in your hand.

手の中に持っているものを見せてください。

➡ この what は先行詞を含む関係代名詞。

◆that の特別用法

先行詞に all, the only, the same, the first, the last, 最上級などがついたときに that はよく使われる。

He is the first boy that came into the room.

彼は部屋に入ってきた最初の少年です。

You are the only man that I can call my friend.

君は僕が友達とよべる唯一の人だ。

◆非制限用法の関係代名詞

補助的説明を加える用法を非制限的用法といい，コンマをつける。

My sister, who is crazy about dancing, is good at English.

私の唯一の姉はダンスにはまっているが英語は得意だ。

My sister who is crazy about dancing is good at English.

ダンスにはまっている姉は英語が得意だ。

➡ 後者は，他に姉妹がいることを示している。

■間接疑問文

Can you show me where the lump is?

➡ show は show + O_1 + O_2 で使ってあるので，where the lump is は Where is the lump? が形を変えて O_2 になっている。疑問符がついたほうを直接疑問文。疑問符をとって語順を変えたものを間接疑問文。

Where is the station? を間接疑問文に変えると where the station is となり，もとの文の O_2 に入れると，Can you show me where the station is?（駅はどこか教えてください）となる。I know how old she is. は，彼女が何歳か私は知っている。

Tell me when she will leave for Australia.（いつ彼女はオーストラリアに出発するのか教えて）のように使える。語順が変わらないのもある。たとえば，

What made her angry?　なにが彼女を怒らせたの？ → なぜ彼女は怒っていたの？　つまり，直接疑問文が SV の語順になっていれば間接疑問文は語順を変える操作をしなくてもいい。

I didn't know what made her angry.

私は彼女がなぜ怒ったのかわかりませんでした。

■助動詞 can

①**可能**　I can swim.　私は泳ぐことができる。

②**可能性**　He can still be at home.　彼はまだ家にいるかもしれない。

③**強い疑問**　Can it be true?　いったいそれは本当かしら。

④**否定の確定推量**　Such a thing can't be true.　そんなことが本当のはずがない。She can't have done such a thing.　彼女がそんなことをしたはずがない。

⑤**許可**　Can I have this cake?　このケーキ食べていい。

■受身と使役動詞

「私は財布を盗まれた」を，I was stolen my wallet. とする間違いが多い。steal は「～を盗む」なので Someone stole my wallet. → My wallet was stolen by someone. が受け身文になる。使役動詞を使うと，I had my wallet stolen. となる。人を主語にして「～を盗まれた」としたいときは，be robbed を使う。She was robbed of some jewels.　彼女は宝石類を盗まれた。

theme 9 Blood Pressure

D : Doctor　P : Patient

(At the end of the exam)

D : Your (a) is a little high.

P : Is it dangerously high?

D : Any time it's high, it's something to worry about. Your (b) doesn't help it. I'd like to see you lose (c).

P : I hate diets.

D : Well, I'd like you to meet with (d). She can (e) some changes in what you eat. Rice (f) potatoes, for example.

P : Hmmm.

D : And alcohol. (g).

P : What else?

D : You should (h) on salt and caffeine. Try drinking decaffeinated coffee and juice instead of coke.

P : It sounds like a lot of changes.

D : Yes, but (i) you'll get used to these new foods, and (j) you'll be better off.

設問 上の会話文の空所（a）～（j）に入れる最も適切な語句を下の①～⑩の中から１つずつ選びなさい。

① weight　② suggest　③ a nutritionist　④ blood pressure
⑤ cut down　⑥ in the long run　⑦ The less, the better
⑧ twenty pounds　⑨ instead of　⑩ after a while

語句解説

- **blood pressure**　血圧
- **dangerously**　副 危険なくらい　形 **dangerous**　危険な　名 **danger**　危険
- any time ➡ この文では接続詞的に「～するときはいつも」という意味。whenever より口語的，接続詞的に使うときは any time と 2 語でつづるが，副詞的に「いつでも」の意味のときは 1 語つづりで anytime = at any time を用いる。
- Your weight doesn't help it. ➡ この help は「～をよくする，治す，促進（助長）する」。**it = high blood pressure**　あなたの体重が血圧を悪くしている → 体重がよくないですね
- **I'd like to see you lose twenty pounds.**　20ポンド軽くなったあなたを見てみたい。→ 20ポンド減量してほしいですね。would like to = want to の丁寧な表現。
- **I hate diets.**　私はダイエット（規定食）は大嫌いです。➡ hate は dislike より強意。**diet**（体重を増やすためや病気を治すための）規定食
- **would like** Ⓐ **to do～**　Ⓐ に～してほしい = **want** Ⓐ **to do～**

  I'd like you to meet with a nutritionist.

  私はあなたに栄養士に会ってもらいたい。

  nutritionist = an expert in nutrition　栄養士

  nutrition　栄養学／**nutritional**　栄養学の／**nutritious**　栄養のある
- **instead of**　～の代わりに，～しないで

  I can walk to work instead of going by car.　車ではなく歩いて仕事に行ける。
- **The less, the better.**　少なければ少ないほどいい。

  The + 比較級～，the + 比較級……「～すればするほど……」

  The more I thought about it, the more depressed I became.

  そのことについて考えれば考えるほど私は落ち込んだ。
- **cut down on～**　～の量（数）を減らす　**The doctor told him to cut down on his drinking.**　医者は彼に酒を減らすようにと言った。
- **decaffeinated coffee**　カフェイン抜きのコーヒー
- **get used to + 名詞**　～に慣れる
- **in the long run**　長期的には ⇔ **in the short run**　短期的には
- **be better off**　よりよい状態である（幸せ，健康面で）➡ be well off が原級。

  She is better off without him.　彼女は彼がいなくても大丈夫だ。

解答はp.61

テーマ 9 血　圧

医：医者　患：患者

（検査が終わって）

医：血圧が少し高いですね。

患：危険なほど高いですか。

医：高いときはいつも心配すべきことがあります，体重がよくないですね。20ポンドは軽くしてもらわないと……。

患：ダイエットは嫌いなんです。

医：困りましたね。栄養士を紹介します。食事についていくつかの改善点を挙げてくれるでしょう。たとえば，ポテトの代わりにお米をとるとか……。

患：うむ……。

医：またお酒です。少なければ少ないほどいいんです。

患：他には。

医：塩分やカフェインの摂取量は減らすようにしたほうがいいでしょう。カフェインの入っていないコーヒーとかコーラの代わりにジュースを飲むようにしてください。

患：大変な変更に聞こえますが……。

医：はい。でもしばらくして新しい食べ物に慣れてくると，長期的には改善するでしょう。

解答

（a）④　（b）①　（c）⑧　（d）③　（e）②　（f）⑨　（g）⑦
（h）⑤　（i）⑩　（j）⑥

解説

(a) high から blood pressure を選ぶ。

(b) あなたのなにが血圧を高くしているのかと考えれば，weight がいい。

(c) lose の目的語をさがすと twenty pounds。

(d) 誰に会ってほしいかを考えれば，栄養士 nutritionist。

(e) can のあとなので動詞の原形がくる。suggest と cut down しかないので意味から suggest を選ぶ。

(f) A instead of B がここでは使えそうだ。

(g) 医者の suggestion のなかで，The less, the better. がここには入る。

(h) should のあとなので動詞の原形がくる。cut down しかない。

(i)（j）には，「このような食事に慣れるでしょう」「改善するでしょう」の文から考えて「しばらくしたら」の after a while が（i）に，「長期的にみて」の in the long run が（j）に入る。

文法 語法

■比較を使った重要構文

①The 比較級…, the 比較級～「…すればするほどますます～」

The better I got to know her, the less I liked her.

彼女のことを知れば知るほど好きでなくなった。

The more, the better.　多ければ多いほどいい。

The sooner, the better.　早ければ早いほどいい。

②比較級 and 比較級「ますます～」

The world is getting smaller and smaller.

世界はますます狭くなってきている。

③(all) the＋比較級＋because [for]～「～なのでいっそう…」

I like him all the better because he has human weakness.

＝I like him all the better for his human weakness.

彼は人間的弱さをもっているがゆえにそれだけいっそう私は彼が好きだ。

④none the 比較級＋because [for]～「～だけれどもやはり…」

I love her none the less for her faults.

＝I love her none the less because she has faults.

彼女には欠点もあるがそれでも大好きだ。

⑤know better than to～「～するほどばかではない，～しないくらいの分別がある」

He knows better than to do such a thing.

彼はそんなことをするようなばかではない。

⑥ ● no more than＝only「わずか，～しか」

I have no more than $100.　100ドルしか持っていない。

● not more than＝at most「せいぜい，多くても」

I have not more than $100.　せいぜい100ドルくらいしか持っていない。

● no less than＝as many as／as much as「～も」

I have no less than $100.　100ドルも持っている。

● not less than＝at least「少なくとも」

I have not less than $100.　少なくとも100ドルは持っている。

- **no more～than…＝not～any more than…「～でないのは…でないのと同じだ」**

  A whale is no more a fish than a horse is.

  鯨が魚でないのは馬がそうでないのと同じだ。

- **no less～than…＝just as～as…「…とまったく同じほど～である」**

  She is no less beautiful than her sister.　彼女は姉に劣らず美しい。

⑦ ● **肯定文～, still [much] more…「～まして…はもちろんだ」**

  She can speak French, still more English.

  彼女はフランス語も話す。まして英語はもちろんだ。

- **否定文～, still [much] less…「～ない。ましてもちろん…ない」**

  She can't speak English, still less French.

  彼女は英語も話せない。ましてフランス語などもちろん話せない。

■原級・比較級・最上級の書き換え

◆富士山の構文

Mt. Fuji is the highest mountain in Japan.

富士山は日本で1番高い山だ。

Mt. Fuji is higher than any other mountain in Japan.

富士山は日本の他のどの山より高い。

No（other）mountain in Japan is higher than Mt. Fuji.

富士山より高い山は（他に）日本にはない。

No（other）mountain in Japan is so high as Mt. Fuji.

富士山ほど高い山は（他に）日本にはない。

Mt. Fuji is as high as any（other）mountain in Japan.

富士山は日本の（他の）どの山よりも劣らず高い。

theme 10 A Change of Hospital Rooms

N1 : Nurse 1　N2 : Nurse 2

N1 : Where's Mrs. Benson? I've just been to 401 but she's not there.

N2 : She's been moved.

N1 : When?

N2 : Just a little while ago. Dr. Thomas decided she didn't need to be here.

N1 : Well, (1) I'm supposed to give her a shot at 4 p.m. Where is she?

N2 : 310. But you'd better check her chart. (2) He may have changed the orders.

N1 : I wish someone (　a　) me.

N2 : Dr. Thomas is pretty busy today.

N1 : Are you sure about the room?

N2 : Let's see…yes, 310.

N1 : He never seems to be very considerate (　b　) nurses here. He never explains matters or his wishes too well.

N2 : That's true. But (3) if I were in your shoes, I wouldn't complain to anyone. He's pretty well respected (　c　) here.

設問 上の会話文を読んで次の設問に答えなさい。

1 下線部（1）～（3）をそれぞれ日本語に訳しなさい。

2 空所（a）～（c）に入る単語を下の①～⑨から１つずつ選びなさい。

① in　② to　③ around　④ into　⑤ about

⑥ of　⑦ told　⑧ have told　⑨ had told

語句解説

- She's been moved. = She has been moved. ➡ この move は「～を移す，～を移動する」という意味の他動詞。現在完了形の受身になっているので，「彼女はちょうど移されました」→「彼女は病室が変更になりました」となる。
- **just a little while ago**　ちょっと前に
- **decide（that）～**　～と決める
- **I'm supposed to give her a shot at 4 p.m.**
  私は彼女に午後4時に注射をすることになっている。
  be supposed to　～することになっている
- **you'd better check her chart.**
  あなたは彼女のカルテをチェックしたほうがいい。
  had better～　したほうがいい
  chart = a medical record = a clinical record　カルテ
- **He may have changed the orders.**　彼は指示を変えたかもしれません。
  ➡ **may have + 過去分詞**　～したかもしれない，orders = instructions
- I wish someone had told me. は I wish のあとに仮定法過去完了がきた文。
  I wish + 仮定法過去　～であればいいのになあ
  I wish + 仮定法過去完了　～だったらよかったのになあ
- **be sure about～**　～は確かである
- **Let's see.** ➡ ためらいの表現で，wellと同じように使う。「ええ～と，あ～」
- **be considerate of**　～に対して思いやりがある
- **if I were in your shoes, I wouldn't complain to anyone.** ➡ 仮定法過去の文。
  もし私があなたの立場なら，誰にも不満は言わないでしょう。
  ➡ complain about A to B 「A のことで B に不満を言う」
  この文では about A の部分が省略されている。
  be in one's shoes　人の身になってみる
- **pretty well**　かなりよく

解答はp.67

テーマ 10 病室の変更

看1：看護師1　看2：看護師2

看1：ベンソンさんはどこにいますか。401号室に行ってみたけど彼女がいないんです。

看2：彼女は病室が変更になりましたよ。

看1：いつですか。

看2：ちょっと前です。トーマス先生が彼女はそこにいる必要はないと決めたんです。

看1：私は彼女に4時に注射をすることになっているんです。彼女はどこにいますか。

看2：310号室です。でもカルテをチェックしたほうがいいですよ。彼は指示を変えたかもしれませんから。

看1：誰か教えてくれればよかったのに。

看2：トーマス先生はとても忙しいのよ。

看1：(310号室という) 部屋は間違いありませんね。

看2：ええと…。はい，間違いありません。310号室です。

看1：彼はここの看護師にあまり思いやりがあるようには見えないわ。説明も十分でなければ希望も伝えないし…。

看2：そうですね。でも私があなたの立場なら誰にも不満は言わないわ。彼はここではとても尊敬されている先生だから。

解答

1 （1）私は4時に彼女に注射をすることになっているんです。

（2）彼は指示を変えたかもしれません。

（3）もし私があなたの立場なら誰にも不満は言わないでしょう。

2 (a) ⑨　(b) ⑥　(c) ③

解説

1 (1) be supposed to「～することになっている」，と give + O_1 + O_2「O_1 に O_2 をあげる」が訳出のポイント。

(2) may have p.p.「～したかもしれない」
orders は医者の指示・命令。＝instructions

(3) 仮定法過去の文なので，そこをうまく訳したい。
If S_1 + 動詞の過去形～，S_2 + 助動詞の過去形…
「S_1 が～なら S_2 は…だろう」

2 (a) I wish のあとの形を考えると⑦か⑨，ここでは文脈から「教えてくれればよかったのに」となるから仮定法過去完了形をえらぶ。

(b) be considerate of　～のことを慮（おもんぱか）る，～に対して思いやりがある

(c) around here　ここらあたりでは，ここでは

文法 語法

■be supposed to の語法

①～するものと思われている

He is supposed to be a good student.　彼はいい学生と思われている。

②～することになっている，～しなければならない

You are supposed to study every night.
あなたは毎晩勉強することになっている。

You are not supposed to smoke in this room.
この部屋ではたばこを吸ってはいけません。

✎ not とともに使うと婉曲的な禁止表現になる。

■助動詞＋have＋過去分詞（p.p.）

may have p.p.　～したかもしれない，**must have p.p.**　～したに違いない，**cannot have p.p.**　～したはずがない，**should have p.p.**　～すべきだったのに…，**shouldn't have p.p.**　～すべきではなかったのに…，**need have p.p.**　～する必要があったのに…，**needn't have p.p.**　～する必要はなかったのに…

He must have passed the exam because he looks happy.
彼はうれしそうに見えるから試験に受かったに違いない。

He should have visited her.　彼は彼女を訪問すべきだったのに。

You needn't have brought your umbrella.
君は傘を持ってくる必要はなかったのに。

■仮定法

◆**仮定法過去**（現在の事実と違うことの仮定とそれをもとにした仮想）

If S_1＋動詞の過去形～，S_2＋助動詞の過去形＋動詞の原形…

「もし S_1 が～なら，S_2 は…だろう」

If I knew her address, I could write to her.
彼女の住所を知っていれば手紙が書けるのになあ。

＝As I don't know her address, I can't write to her.
　彼女の住所を知らないので手紙が書けません。

◆**仮定法過去完了**（過去の事実と違うことの仮定とそれをもとにした仮想）

If S_1＋had＋動詞の過去分詞〜，S_2＋助動詞の過去形＋have＋動詞の過去分詞…「もし S_1 が〜だったら，S_2 は…だっただろう」

If I had known her address then, I could（would）have written to her.

彼女の住所をその時知っていたら手紙を書いたのになあ。

＝As I didn't know her address then, I couldn't write to her.

彼女の住所を知らなかったので手紙を書けませんでした。

◆**仮定法未来**（should と were to を使った仮定法）

ありそうもないことの仮定，絶対にありえないことの仮定に使われる。

If S should＋動詞の原形〜,…「万一Sが〜したら，…」

If he should come here, please give him this letter.

万一彼が来たら，この手紙を彼に渡してください。

If S_1 were to 動詞の原形〜，S_2＋動詞の過去形＋動詞の原形…

「仮に S_1 が〜したら S_2 は…だろう」

If I were to tell you the truth, you would be surprised.

もし私が真実を話したらあなたは驚くでしょう。

■I wish＋仮定法「〜いいなあ，〜だったらよかったなあ」

I wish I were rich.　金持ちだったらいいのになあ。

I wish I had followed his advice.　彼の助言に従っていたらなあ。

■It's time＋仮定法過去「そろそろ〜する時間だ」

It's about time you went to bed.

＝It's about time for you to go to bed.　そろそろ寝る時間ですよ。

この構文では about の代わりに high や almost が使える。

theme 11 A Medication Question

P : Patient　Ph : Pharmacist

P　: Do you have generic medicine for this prescription?

Ph : Yes, this one costs $15. Just a moment. I'll be back soon.

(Later)

Ph : Here you are. Take it three times a day with meals.

P　: Before or after?

Ph : With or after. Take it on an empty stomach and you might feel a little nauseous. [(1)].

P　: Are there any side effects?

Ph : No, but [(2)]. If you're on any medication, alcohol is going to (3) <u>affect</u> it, and maybe (4) <u>decrease</u> the effect you want from the medication.

P　: Can I get a refill?

Ph : Yes, but you'll need a new prescription.

設問 上の会話文を読んで次の設問に答えなさい。

1 空所（1）（2）に入る文章を，単語を並べ替えて意味の通る文章にしなさい。

（1） and, directions, stick, fine, you'll, to, be, the

（2） get, might, alcohol, or, avoid, you, drowsy

2 下線部（3）の同意語，（4）の反意語を次の語群の中からそれぞれ選びなさい。

（A） reduce　（B） avoid　（C） influence　（D） increase

（E） affection　（F） defect

語句解説

- **generic medicine**　後発医薬品（開発費がかかっていないので先発医薬品より安い）
- **cost**（費用が）～かかる
- **Here you are.**　はいどうぞ。➡ なにか物を差し出すときの表現。他に，Here it is. がある。前者が人に，後者が物に重点をおいた表現。
- **a day＝per day**　１日当たり／**twice a day**　１日2回
- **empty stomach**　空っぽの胃袋 → 空きっ腹
- **nauseous**　㊂吐き気がする／**feel (get) a little nauseous**　ちょっと吐き気がする
- **stick to＋O**　Oを固守する ➡ 本文では O が the directions なので「使用法通りにする」が適訳。
- **directions**　使用法，説明書き
- **side effects**　副作用
- **avoid**　～を避ける＝**evade**
- **drowsy**　㊂眠い，眠気を誘う／**get drowsy**　眠くなる
- **medication**　薬物治療，薬物
- **affect**　～に影響を与える＝**influence**
  His opinion affected my decision.　彼の意見に私の決断は影響をうけた。
- **effect**　効果，結果
  This medicine had no effect on me.　この薬はまったく効かなかった。
- **decrease**　～を減らす，～が減る，減少 ⇔ **increase**　～を増やす，～が増える，増加
  The number of students has markedly decreased.
  学生の数はめっきり減ってきた。
  This medicine decreases my pain.　この薬は痛みを和らげてくれる。
  The decrease in income affects our lives.
  収入の減少は私達の生活に影響を与える。
- **refill**　再調剤する

解答はp.73

テーマ 11 薬の使いかたについての質問

患：患者　薬：薬剤師

患：この処方薬のジェネリック（ノーブランド薬）ありますか。

薬：はいありますよ。15ドルです。しばらくお待ちください。すぐ戻ります。

（しばらくして）

薬：はいどうぞ。食事と一緒に１日３回飲んでください。

患：食前ですか，食後ですか。

薬：食事中か食後です。空腹時に飲むとちょっと吐き気がするかもしれません。使用法に従っていれば大丈夫です。

患：なにか副作用はありますか。

薬：ありません。でもお酒は避けてください。そうでないと眠気をもよおすことがあります。たとえどんな薬を服用するのでも，アルコールは影響しますから薬の効果は減ってしまいます。

患：再調剤はしてもらえますか。

薬：はい，ただし新しい処方箋(せん)が必要となります。

解答

1 (1) Stick to the directions, and you'll be fine

(2) avoid alcohol, or you might get drowsy

2 (3) − (C)　(4) − (D)

解説

1 (1) 命令文, and～「…しなさい，そうすれば～」，stick to～

(2) 命令文, or～「…しなさい，そうしないと～」，get drowsy がポイント。

2 affect = influence，decrease ⇔ increase

知っておきたいことわざ⑤

□光陰（こういん）矢のごとし

Time flies.／Time has wings.

□人事を尽くして天命を待つ

Do your best and abide by the event.／I take what I get.

文法 語法

■命令文，and～「…しなさい，そうすれば～」

■命令文，or～「…しなさい，そうでないと～」

Work hard, and you'll succeed. = If you work hard, you'll succeed.

一生懸命働きなさい，そうすればうまくいきます。

Hurry up, or you'll be late for school. = If you don't hurry up, you'll be late for school. = Unless you hurry up, you'll be late for school.

急ぎなさい，そうでないと学校に遅れますよ。

■否定命令文／強意の命令文

Don't speak so quickly.　そんなに早口で話さないでくれ。

Never mind!　気にするな。

Do be quiet.　静かにしなさい。

Do listen to me.　私の言うことを聴きなさい。

■受動態の命令文

Do it at once. → Let it be done at once.　すぐにそれをしなさい。

■譲歩を表す特殊な命令文

「たとえ～しても」の意味を表し，「～するならしなさい」から転じたもの。

I'll help you, come what may.　なにが起ころうと君を助けましょう。

■不定冠詞 a, an の語法

① **1つの**　I have a cat.　私は猫を１匹飼っている。

② **～につき**　He earns ten million yen a year.　彼の年収は１千万円だ。

③ **同じ～**　We are of an age.　私たちは同じ年だ。

④ **～という人**　A Mr. Smith came to see you while you were out.
留守中にスミスさんという方がいらっしゃいました。

⑤ **～のような人**　He thinks he is an Einstein.
彼は自分をアインシュタインのような偉大な学者だと思っている。

患者の使う決まり文句（症状の表現）③

I had a rash on my face.

顔に発疹ができました。

I've got little spots all over my body.

私は身体中小さなぶつぶつができました。

I have a rash all over my body.

身体中に発疹ができました。

I am allergic to peanuts and so when I eat some I break out in hives.

ピーナツのアレルギーなので食べるとじんましんが出ます。

I have the cramps. ／ I have bad menstrual pain.

生理痛がひどいんです。

I have difficulty swallowing.

物を飲み込むのが大変です。

I feel so tired and weak lately.

最近疲れがひどく身体が弱ってきました。

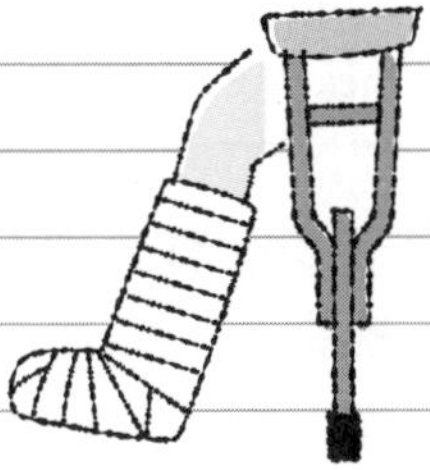

I have no interest in anything these days.

この頃なにもする気が起きません。

I slipped on the stairs and injured my ankle.

階段ですべって足首を痛めました。

My feet are swollen.

足がむくんでいます。

I feel gassy. ＝ I feel bloated. ＝ My stomach feels bloated.

お腹が張った感じがする。

I had blood in my stool.　下血しました。

I can't have a bowel movement.　便通がありません。

I've got constipation recently.　最近便秘ぎみです。

theme 12 Teeth Cleaning

D.H. : Dental Hygienist　P : Patient　H : Dr.Hanks

D.H. : How are you today, Mr. Willis?

P　: I'm O.K.

D.H. : Just （ 1 ） back and （ 2 ） wide.

P　: (a) Aren't I going to see Dr. Hanks?

D.H. : A little later. First I'll （ 3 ） some cleaning, and then Dr. Hanks will （ 4 ） you.

P　: What if I （ 5 ） a cavity?

D.H. : Well, she will （ 6 ） to you about that, and that's what I'll （ 7 ） looking for.

(Later)

H　: (b) It looks like you've got a few cavities, Mr. Willis.

P　: Hmm. Well, I'm a little busy today. Can I （ 8 ） an appointment for next week?

設問 上の会話文を読んで次の設問に答えなさい。

1. 下線部 (a) (b) を日本語に訳しなさい。
2. 空所 (1) ～ (8) に入る適切な動詞を下の語群から選びなさい。

do	go	make	see	be	sit
close	open	have	tell	talk	

語句解説

- **teeth cleaning**　歯のクリーニング
- **dental hygienist**　歯科衛生技師
- **How are you today, Mr. Willis?**　今日はどんな具合ですか。→ こんにちは，ウイルスさん。
- **sit back**（椅子などに）ゆったりと座る
- **Aren't I going to see Dr. Hanks?**
  私はハンクス先生に診てもらうことになっていないのですか。
  ➡ aren't は ain't も使える。amn't がないので I に対しても aren't を使う。
  be going to　～することになっている＝確定した予定
- **What if～?**　～したらどうなるだろうか。
  What if he comes to see us today?　彼が今日会いにやって来たらどうしよう。
  ➡ What if he came to see us today? となったら comes より came のほうが遠まわしの表現になる。
- **cavity**　虫歯（の穴）＝**a cavity in a tooth**／**a decayed tooth**　虫歯
- **that's what I'll be looking for**　それが，私がこれから見つけようとしていることです ➡ この what は関係代名詞。
- **look like**　～のようである
  ➡ like が接続詞で使われて，あとに you've got a few cavities という節が続いている。
- have got＝have
- **make an appointment**　予約を入れる

解答はp.79

テーマ 12 歯のクリーニング

歯：歯科衛生技師　患：患者　ハ：ハンクス歯科医

歯：ウイルスさん，こんにちは。
患：こんにちは。
歯：腰かけて口を大きく開けてください。
患：ハンクス先生に診てもらうんじゃないんですか。
歯：あとでです。私がまず初めにきれいにしてから，ハンクス先生が診てくれますよ。
患：虫歯があったらどうしましょうか。
歯：そうですね。先生がそのことについては話してくれます。それがこれから私がやろうとしていることです。
（しばらくして）
ハ：2，3本虫歯があるようですね，ウイルスさん。
患：うむ。今日はちょっと忙しいので，来週予約入れてもらえますか。

解答

1 (a) ハンクス先生に診てもらうんじゃないんですか。

(b) 2，3本虫歯があるようですね。

2 (1) sit (2) open (3) do (4) see (5) have (6) talk
(7) be (8) make

解説

1 (a) **be going to** ～するつもり（確定した予定），**see**（医者に）診てもらう
➡ amn't という短縮形がないので，主語が I であるにもかかわらず aren't を使ってある。

(b) **look like** ～のように見える，**you've got＝you have got** あなたは～をもっている
have got＝have，cavity は虫歯。

2 歯医者での会話なので，(1)(2)にはそれぞれ sit と open が入れられるだろう。(3)は cleaning から考えて do，(4)はハンクス先生があなたを診るんだから see，(5)は虫歯があったらどうしようという文脈から have，(6)には to があるから talk to がいい，(7)は未来進行形だから be，(8)は appointment からみて make がくる。

文法 語法

■挨拶の表現（元気？／どうしてる？　など）

◆How 型

How are you?／How are you doing?／How's it going?／How's everything?／How are things?　など。

答えかたは，Good.／Great.／Fine.　など。

◆What 型

What's up?／What's new?／What's happening?　など。

答えかたは，Not much.（別に）。

他に具体的に，I've been so busy.／I moved into a new apartment.　など。

■否定疑問文に対する答えかた

Aren't you a student? のような否定疑問文の答えかたで，日本語の「はい，違います」とか「いいえ，そうです」にひきずられて，Yes, I'm not. とか No, I am. になりがちだがこれは間違い。否定疑問文であろうがその他の疑問文であろうが，学生か学生でないかを尋ねているので，事実が学生ならば Yes, I am. 学生でなければ，No, I'm not. となる。

以下のどの疑問文の形式で尋ねられても答えかたは同じと考えればよい。

You are a student?／You aren't a student?／You are a student, aren't you?／You aren't a student, are you?／Are you a student?／Aren't you a student?

■Like の語法

動詞の like 以外に like にはいろいろな用法がある。

前置詞として：He is like his father.　彼は父親似だ。／He looks like an actor.　彼は役者のように見える。／What is she like?　彼女はどんな人ですか。

接続詞として：You look like you had a dreadful dream.　君は怖い夢を見たようですね。／I can't do it like you do.　私は君のするようにはできない。

■Make がつくる動詞句［make＋a（an）＋名詞］

動詞１語でいうより口語的になる。さらに名詞に形容詞をつけることもできる。たとえば，**make an early start**（早く出発する），**make no mistake**（失敗をしない）。その他，

make an appointment　予約する，**make a plan**　計画を立てる，**make a start**　出発する，**make an offer**　申し出る，**make a reservation**　予約する，**make a request**　要求する，**make a suggestion**　提案する，**make a difference**　違いがある・重要である，**make a mistake**　間違いをする，**make a joke**　冗談を言う，**make a study**　研究をする，**make a sound**　音を立てる

■do がつくる動詞句

do the dishes　皿洗いをする，**do one's teeth**　歯を磨く，**do one's hair**　髪を整える，**do the flowers**　花を生ける，**do the room**　部屋を掃除する，**do a manzai**　漫才をする，**do the laundry**　洗濯をする

■have の基本は「〜をもっている」

I have a lot of money now.　今，金がたくさんある。

I have no luck.　ついてない。

I had fun.　楽しかった。

I have a bad cold.　ひどい風邪をひいている。

I have faith in God.　神を信じている。

I have to stop smoking.　たばこをやめなければいけない。

I have my hair cut.　髪を切る（切ってもらう）。

I'll have him call you back.　彼に折り返し電話をさせます。

I'd like to have a cup of tea.　お茶を1杯いただきたい。

theme 13 Visiting Hours

R : Patient's Relative　N : Nurse

R : Excuse me, where is Room 401. [(a)].

N : I'm sorry. Visiting hours are from 1:00 to 8:00. It's now eleven thirty. [(b)].

R : But [(c)].

N : [(d)]. If you want to have lunch in the coffee shop, you might be able to see her a little early.

R : But [(A)].

N : [(e)]. Parents of new babies can come anytime.

設問 上の会話文を読んで次の設問に答えなさい。

1 空所（a）～（e）に入る文を下の①～⑤から１つずつ選びなさい。

① I'd really like to see her

② I'd like to see my aunt

③ I understand, but those are the rules

④ I'm afraid you'll have to wait

⑤ He's probably a new father

2 空所（A）に「私は先ほど男の人が奥さんに会いに行くのを見ました」という意味の英文がくるように単語を並べ替えて正しい英文にしなさい。

go	saw	see	ago	wife	I
a	man	a	his	minute	

語句解説

- **Excuse me,~**　すみません。／ごめんください。➡ 未知の人に話しかけたり，人の前を通ったり，その他失礼にあたる行為に対する詫(わ)びのことば。
  Excuse me, sir, what time is it now?　すみません。今何時でしょうか。
  Excuse me, but would you show me the way to the station?
  すみませんが，駅までの道を教えてください。
- **I'm sorry.**　残念です。／お気の毒に思います。
- **visiting hours**　面会時間
- **I'm afraid~**　（よくないことを言うとき）～と思う
  I'm afraid it'll rain tomorrow.　残念ながら明日は雨のようです。
- **those are the rules**　それは決まりです
- **go see＝go to see＝go and see**　会いに行く，面会に行く
  come see＝come to see＝come and see　会いに来る
  Come see me tomorrow.　明日会いに来てね。
- **a new father**　（子どもが生まれて）新しく父親になった人
- **new babies**　生まれたばかりの赤ちゃん＝新生児
- **anytime＝at any time**　いつでも

解答はp.85

テーマ 13 面会時間

身：患者の身内　看：看護師

身：すみませんが401号室はどちらでしょうか。おばに会いたいのですが…。

看：残念ですが，面会時間は１時から８時までです。今まだ11時半です。待ってもらわなくてはなりません。

身：でもおばに本当に会いたいのです。

看：わかりますけど，決まりですから。喫茶店でお昼を食べてれば，少しは早くおばさんに会えるかもしれませんよ。

身：でも，男の人がちょっと前に奥さんに面会に行くのを見ましたよ。

看：その人はたぶんお父さんになったばかりの人です。新しく生まれた赤ちゃんの両親はいつでも会えるんです。

解答 ●●

1 (a) ② (b) ④ (c) ① (d) ③ (e) ⑤

2 I saw a man go see his wife a minute ago

解説 ●●

1 対話文の冒頭部分と選択肢から,「おばさんに会いたい」と言ったのに対して,「面会時間じゃないので待たなくてはいけません」と看護師に言われたが「でも本当に会いたいんです」とねばる場面だから, (a)(b)(c) に②④①の順で入るのは容易だろう。残りの (d)(e) には, 流れから,「規則だから」の③が先にくる。

2 ポイントは, 知覚動詞 see ＋ 人 ＋ do（原形動詞）「人 が～するのを見かける」と, go see ＋ 人「人 に会いに行く」。

I saw a man go see his wife a minute ago.

The man went see his wife. その男の人は妻に会いに行った。

知っておきたいことわざ⑥

□天は自ら助くる者を助く

Heaven helps those who help themselves.

□言うは易し行うは難し

Easier said than done.

Who will bell the cat? (誰が猫に鈴をつけるのか) bell 鈴をつける

文法 語法

■I'm afraid～／I hope～の構文

残念ながら～と思う ⇔ ～と希望する

I'm afraid you are to blame for it.　残念ながらそれはあなたが悪いと思う。

I hope it will be fine tomorrow.　明日天気だといいですね。

■I'm afraid so. I'm afraid not.／I hope so. I hope not.

Will it rain tomorrow?　明日は雨でしょうか。

I'm afraid so. = I'm afraid it will rain tomorrow.

残念ながらどうもそのようです。

I'm afraid not. = I'm afraid it won't rain tomorrow.

残念ながら明日も雨には恵まれません。

I hope so. = I hope it will rain tomorrow.　そうなることを希望します。

I hope not. = I hope it won't rain tomorrow.　そうならないことを希望します。

■知覚動詞の用法

see, look at, watch, hear, listen to, feel, notice, smell　など。

知覚動詞 + 目的語 + 現在分詞

I felt the ground trembling.　地面が揺れているのが感じられた。

知覚動詞 + 目的語 + 原形不定詞

I saw a stranger enter his house.

見知らぬ人物が彼の家に入るのが見えた。

知覚動詞 + 目的語 + 過去分詞

I saw the boy carried to the hospital.

私はその男の子が病院に運ばれるのを見ました。

医者・看護師が使う決まり文句①

What seems to be the problem? どんな具合ですか。

What can I do for you? どうしました。

What are your symptoms? なにか症状がありますか。

Well, now, how can I help you? さて今回はどうなさいましたか。

Well, Mr.Smith, what's the trouble?
さて，スミスさん，どうなさいましたか。

What brings you in to see the doctor? 今日はどうなさいました。

Here is a questionnaire that should be completed and returned to me, Mr.Smith. スミスさん，この用紙の各項目に記入して書き終わりましたら私にください。

I will weigh you first. まず体重をはかります。

Let me take your pulse and blood pressure.
血圧と脈拍をとらせてください。

Let me listen to your lungs. 聴診器をあててみますね。

Please lie on your tummy. 腹ばいになってください。

Please turn over and lie on your back.
向きを変えて仰向けになってください。

Take a deep breath. 深呼吸をしてください。

I am going to check your blood pressure. 血圧をはかります。

Let me try your blood pressure. Very good. 160 over 105.
血圧をはかりましょう。いいですね。上が160で下が105です。

Your blood pressure reading is high. 血圧が高いですね。

Is there a family history of high blood pressure?
高血圧の家系ですか。

I want to run some tests. いくつかテストをします。

I'll take a blood sample from your arm. 腕から血液を採ります。

theme 14 A Child Getting a Shot

N : Nurse　B : Brian　M : Mother

N : Hello, Brian. Are you going to be brave today?

B : (silence)

M : (　　a　　)

B : (　　b　　)

N : (　　c　　)

B : (　　d　　)

N : (　　e　　) I don't think it will hurt. Maybe it'll sting for a few seconds, but I bet you'll be brave. Can you roll up your sleeve?

B : (　　f　　)

M : Well, try to be brave and afterwards we'll get some ice cream.

設問 上の会話文の空所（a）～（f）に入る適当な文を次の①～⑥から１つずつ選びなさい。

① I'll try to be gentle.

② He'll try.

③ But I'm scared.

④ Will it hurt?

⑤ Why do I have to get a shot?

⑥ So you won't get sick.

語句解説

- shot = injection　注射
- brave　勇敢な，勇気のある

Are you going to be brave today?

今日は勇敢でいられるかな。→ 今日は注射大丈夫かな。

- gentle　やさしい
- sting　刺す，ズキズキ痛む
- I bet ～　きっと～だ

I bet you'll be brave.　ブライアンならきっと勇敢でいられると思うわ。→ ブライアンならきっと我慢できるわ。

- roll up one's sleeve　そでをまくり上げる，腕まくりする
- scare　動 ～を怖がらせる ➡ be scared で，～を怖がる，～をおびえる

I'm scared.　怖いんだよ。／**I'm scared of snakes.**　私はへびが怖い。／**I'm scared to death.**　死ぬほど怖い。

- try to be brave　頑張ってみてね
- afterwards　あとで
- we'll get some ice cream.　私達はアイスクリームを買います。→ アイスクリーム買ってあげるからね。

解答はp.91

テーマ 14 注射をうける子ども

看：看護師　ブ：ブライアン　母：母親

看：こんにちは，ブライアン。今日注射は大丈夫かな。

ブ：（沈黙）

母：彼はやりますよ。

ブ：なぜ注射しなくちゃいけないの。

看：病気にかからないようによ。

ブ：痛い？

看：やさしくするから痛くないわよ。ちょっとちくっとするけどブライアンならきっと我慢できるわ。そでをまくってくれる。

ブ：でも怖いんだ。

母：我慢したら，あとでアイスクリーム買ってあげるわよ。

解答

(a) ② (b) ⑤ (c) ⑥ (d) ④ (e) ① (f) ③

解説

注射をうける子どもをなだめすかしている場面。Are you going to be brave today?（今日は，注射は大丈夫かな）に対して，ブライアンが沈黙するが，代わりに母親が He'll try.（大丈夫ですよ）と応える。次は，Why に対して，So〜. で応えるのと，Will it hurt?（痛い？）に対して I'll try to be gentle.（やさしくするね）で応えるのが組み合わせられればいい。

知っておきたいことわざ⑦

□千里の道も一歩から

Little by little one goes far.

□虎穴（こけつ）に入（い）らずんば虎児（こじ）を得ず

Nothing venture, nothing gain.

Nothing ventured, nothing gained.

文法 語法

■現在分詞

現在分詞は分詞形容詞として前からも後ろからも修飾できる。また，叙述的な用法としても使える。

a singing girl 歌っている少女／**a girl dancing to the music** 音楽に合わせて踊っている少女／**Give me an interesting book.** 面白い本を貸してください。**The book is interesting.** その本は面白い。／**She sat reading the book.** 彼女はその本を読みながら座っていた。／**I saw her singing with a boy.** 彼女が男の子と歌っているのが見えた。

■I bet～／You bet～「きっと～だ」

You bet.＝No problem.＝Sure.＝Certainly.「もちろんいいよ，もちろん」

I bet［you bet］you'll get some candies from her.

きっと彼女からチョコもらうよ。

Are you nervous?　You bet.　緊張してる？　もちろん！

■受動態で使われる動詞

日本語では能動態で表現するところを英語では受動態でいう。

➡感情を表す他動詞

be surprised（astonished, amazed, astounded）at 驚く，**be satisfied（contented）with** 満足する，**be amused at** 面白がる，**be interested in** 興味がある，**be pleased with** 喜ぶ，**be grieved at** 悲しむ，**be delighted at** 大喜びする，**be disappointed at** 失望する，**be discouraged at** 元気がなくなる，**be ashamed of** 恥じる，**be worried about** 心配する，**be shocked at** ショックを受ける，**be frightened of** 怖がる，**be terrified by** 恐れる・おびえる，**be tired from** 疲れる，**be disgusted at** うんざりする

I was surprised at the news.　そのニュースに驚いた。

I was surprised to hear the news.　そのニュースを聞いて驚いた。

I was surprised by her reaction.　彼女の反応に驚いた。

I'm surprised（that）you're married.　君が既婚者とは驚いた。

➡ 動詞が他動詞として強く意識されると at ではなく by となる。つまり，surprised が形容詞化していなくて，受動的色彩が濃厚なときは by が使われる。

They were amused at her jokes.　彼らは彼女の冗談を面白がった。

She is amused with the new doll.　彼女は新しい人形が気に入っている。

They are worried about the possible spread of the disease.
彼らは病気の拡がりを心配している。

at は動名詞や見たり聞いたりする対象に，with は物や人に，about は事柄に用いる。

➡被害損傷を表す他動詞

be injured（**wounded**）負傷する，**be defeated**　負ける，**be drowned**　溺死（できし）する，**be wrecked**　難破する，**be taken ill**　病気になる，**be killed**　死ぬ，**be delayed**　遅れる

More than three thousand soldiers were killed in the war.
その戦争で3千人以上の兵士が亡くなった。

The train was delayed three hours because of the accident.
電車は事故のために3時間遅れた。

■Why～？に対して So～の答えかた

Why に対して Because ではなく So が使われることもある。これは Why do you go to the library? という問いに対して To study.（勉強するため）のように目的を表す To 不定詞を使うことがあるが，同様に so（that）～「～のため」という目的を表す副詞節が使われていると考えればいい。

Why do I have to get a shot?　So you won't get sick.
なんで注射しなけりゃいけないの。　病気にならないようによ。

Why do you recommend I get married?　So you can save a lot.
なぜ結婚を勧めるの。　節約できるからさ。

theme 15 A Bad Reaction to Medication

M : Mother　N : Nurse

(On the phone)

M : Dr. Harris prescribed (1) <u>an antibiotic</u> (a) my son's ear infection, but I have a few questions (b) it.

N : Sure. What would you like to know?

M : He's been taking it (c) three days, but he doesn't seem any better, and he's very irritable. He won't eat anything.

N : Has he been (d) this medication before?

M : No, never.

N : It could be (2) <u>an allergic reaction</u>. Some people react that way. Why don't you drop (e) and the doctor will have another look (f) him?

設問 上の会話文を読んで次の設問に答えなさい。

1 下線部 (1) (2) の意味を書きなさい。

2 空所 (a) ～ (f) に入る前置詞を下の語群から選びなさい。

on	of	for	at	by	about	up	to

語句解説

- **bad reaction = rejection**　拒絶反応
- **antibiotic**　名 形 抗生物質（の）
- **Sure.**（返答として）いいとも，もちろん
- **He doesn't seem any better.**　彼は全然よくなっているようには見えない。
  ➡ not～any で強い否定の形になっている。
- **irritable**　いらいらした，怒りっぽい，過敏な
- **won't = will not**　～しようとしない
  He won't eat anything.　彼はなにも食べようとしない。
- **It could be～**　～という可能性があるでしょう
  ➡ この could は現在時または未来に対する推量を表す。
- **an allergic reaction**　アレルギー反応
- **Why don't you drop by～?**　立ち寄ってみてください。
  drop by = drop in = stop by　立ち寄る
  Why don't you～?　～しませんか（勧誘の表現）
- **have another look at～**　～をもう１度見る

解答はp.97

テーマ 15 薬に対する拒絶反応

母：母親　看：看護師

（電話で）

母：ハリス先生は息子の耳の病気に抗生物質を処方してくれましたが，それについて２，３質問があります。

看：どうぞ。なにをお聞きになりたいですか。

母：息子は３日間薬を飲んでいますが，全然よくなっているようには見えません。とてもいらいらしています。なにも食べようとしません。

看：以前にこの薬を処方されたことがありますか。

母：いいえ，１度もありません。

看：アレルギー反応かもしれません。そのように反応する人もいます。病院に来てみてください。先生がもう１度診てくれますから。

解答

1 (1) 抗生物質　(2) アレルギー反応

2 (a) for　(b) about　(c) for　(d) on　(e) by　(f) at

解説

1 常識として知っておきたい単語。

2 (a)「～に適した」の意味の前置詞は for。

books for children　子ども向けの本

(b)「～について」about。

a book about flowers　花に関する本

(c)「～の間」期間を表す for。現在完了形と一緒によく使われる。

(d) **be on medication for～**　～に対して薬物療法をうけている

(e) **drop by～**　立ち寄る　**Drop by sometime.**　いつか立ち寄ってね。

(f) **look at～**　～を診る，見る／**have a look at～**　～を見る／

have another look at～　～をもう1度見る

医療福祉系の職業①

□医師	**doctor**（一般に医者），**physician**（内科医），**surgeon**（外科医）
□歯科医師	**dentist**
□看護師	**nurse**
□薬剤師	**pharmacist，chemist**

文法 語法

■勧誘表現

Why don't you（we）～? = Why not～?「～してみたらどうですか」

［口語的表現］

他に，What do you say to～ing? = How（What）about～ing? = Let's～. = Shall we～? などがある。

Why don't you bring him along?　彼を連れてきたらどうですか。

Why don't we have lunch together?　一緒にお昼でもどうですか。

Why not make your lunch instead of buying it?

お昼は買うんじゃなくてつくったらどう？

■固執・拒絶の will not（won't）／would not

He won't do anything.　彼はなにもしようとしない。

He wouldn't do anything.　彼はなにもしようとしなかった。

■可能性・推量の could

Could it be true?　それはいったい本当なの？

The government could do a lot more to help poor people.

政府は貧しい人々を助けるためにもっと多くのことができるだろう。

■another の語法

基本的には an + other だから「他のもう1つ」と考えればいい。

She has another daughter.　彼女にはもう１人娘がいる。

Would you like another cup of coffee?　コーヒーもう１杯いかがですか。

In another two weeks we'll be on holiday.　もう2週間で休みになる。

✎ two weeks を1つのかたまりとして扱う。

One man's meat is another man's poison.（ことわざ）甲の薬は乙の毒

To know is one thing, and to teach is another.

知っていることと教えることとは別のことだ。

医者・看護師が使う決まり文句②

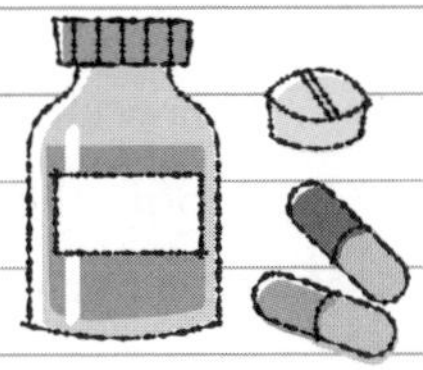

Do you have any problems at home?
家庭でなにか気にかかることがありますか。

Have you been under stress lately at work?
最近，仕事でストレスを感じますか。

Does this hurt?　ここが痛みますか。

Show me where you have been having pain.
どこが痛むか教えてください。

Take off your clothes above the waist. = Strip to the waist.
上衣を脱いでください。

When did this happen?　いつ起こりましたか。

Are you allergic to any medications?
なにかに薬物アレルギーがありますか。

I will prescribe an antibiotic.　抗生物質を処方します。

I'll give you a prescription.　処方箋（せん）を差しあげます。

Try to get plenty of sleep and relax.
十分睡眠をとってリラックスしてください。

I'll listen to your lungs. Take a deep breath and hold. Release now.
肺を診てみましょう。大きく息を吸って，止めてください。はい，吐いて。

I'm going to give you a prescription to take for 7 days.
1週間分の薬の処方箋を書きます。

Be sure to take all the medication.　全部の薬を飲むようにしてください。

I want to see you again in three days.　3日経ったらまた来てください。

Do you have any questions or concerns?
なにか質問か気にかかることがありますか。

How high has your temperature been?　Between 101 and 102.
熱はどのくらいでしょうか。　101から102度の間です。

theme 16 AIDS Warning to a Young Patient

D : Doctor　P : Patient

D : At your age, it's crucial (1) <u>to</u> understand the risks (a) <u>involved</u> with AIDS.

P : Oh, I know all about that.

D : Good. Still, there are certain things I'd like (2) <u>to</u> remind you of, such as safe sex with a condom, and not using needles or drugs at all, of course.

P : Yeah, I know.

D : Well, a lot of people know these things, but they still get (b) <u>infected</u>.

設問 上の会話文を読んで次の設問に答えなさい。

1 下線部（1）（2）の to と同じ使いかたをした文を下の（A）～（E）から1つずつ選びなさい。

(A) He is cruel to do such a thing.

(B) You should follow the directions carefully to get the best results.

(C) For her to succeed is quite certain.

(D) He pretended not to be listening.

(E) I have a lot of books to read.

2 下線部（a）（b）の過去分詞と同じ用法の文を下の①～⑤から選びなさい。

① I didn't hear my name called.

② Bill looked disappointed at her absence.

③ I know the boy named Tom.

④ Left to herself, she began to cry.

⑤ The unexpected has happened.

語句解説

- **AIDS (Acquired Immune Deficiency Syndrome)**　エイズ，後天性免疫不全症候群
- **warning to〜**　〜に対しての警告
- **crucial**　重大な，決定的な
- **risks＜risk**　危険
- **involve**　（人を）〜と関係させる，（人を）〜に巻き込む

  be involved with〜　〜と関係している

  risks involved with AIDS　エイズに巻き込まれる（関係した）危険性
- **still**　（接続詞的に用いて）それでもなお，それでも
- **remind A of B**　AにBを思い出させる

  There are certain things. + **I'd like to remind you of certain things (them).**

  → **There are certain things (that) I'd like to remind you of.**

  あなたに思い出してほしいことがいくつかあります。
- **such as〜**　たとえば〜
- **not〜at all**　全然〜ない＝**by no means**＝**anything but**
- **get infected**　感染する

解答はp.103

テーマ 16 若い患者へのエイズの注意

医：医者　患：患者

医：あなたの年頃では，エイズに感染する危険性を理解するのはとても大事です。

患：えぇ，それについては全部知っています。

医：それはいいことです。でもそれでも気づいてほしいことがいくつかあります。たとえばコンドームを使った安全なセックスはもちろんのことですが注射針や薬物を決して使わないことです。

患：はい，わかっています。

医：多くの人がわかってはいるけど，それでも感染してしまうのです。

解答

1 (1) ー (C)　(2) ー (D)

2 (a) ③　(b) ②

解説

1 (1) It is ～to do…の構文，つまり It＝to 以下，名詞用法の不定詞。

(2) would like to～，like の目的語になっている名詞用法の不定詞。

(A) 彼がそんなことをするなんてむごい。➡ cruel の理由・根拠を表す副詞用法の不定詞。

(B) 最高の結果を出すためにあなたは慎重に指示に従うべきだ。➡「～するため」の目的を表す副詞用法の不定詞。

(C) 彼女が成功することは確実だ。➡ 不定詞の意味上の主語をともなって主語として使われている。名詞用法の不定詞。

(D) 彼は聞いていないふりをした。➡ 動詞 pretend の目的語に使われた名詞用法の不定詞。

(E) 私は読まなければならない本がいっぱいある。➡ books を修飾する形容詞用法の不定詞。

2 (a) はエイズに関係した危険性（リスク），過去分詞が後ろから修飾している。

(b) は感染した状態になる（感染してしまう），become の補語として過去分詞が使われている。

① 私は名前を呼ばれるのが聞こえなかった。➡ hear＋O＋C の C として過去分詞が使われている。

② ビルは彼女の留守にがっかりした様子だった。➡ look＋C の C（補語）として過去分詞が使われている。

③ 私はトムという名前の少年を知っている。➡ named が boy を後ろから修飾している。

④ 彼女は１人にされて泣きだした。➡ As she was left to herself, she began to cry. が分詞構文を使って表現された文。

⑤ 予期せぬことが起こった。➡ The unexpected で予期せぬことという意味の名詞。

文法 語法

■形容詞のはたらきをする過去分詞

a broken vase 壊れた花瓶，**a vase broken by Tom** トムが壊した花瓶，**fallen leaves** 落ち葉，**the boy named Mike** マイクという名の少年，**excited children** わくわくした子どもたち，**an exhausted worker** 疲れきった労働者

Nancy looks delighted.　ナンシーはうれしそうな顔をしている。

I didn't hear my name called.　私は名前が呼ばれるのが聞こえなかった。

He had his license suspended for reckless driving.

彼は無謀（むぼう）運転で免許証を停止された。

I got my work done before noon.　正午前に仕事を終えた。

■It is～to do……の構文

It is～for O to do……／It is ～of O to do……

It is important to learn to speak English.

英語を話せるようになることは大事です。

➡ この it は形式主語の it で to learn to speak English のこと。不定詞の意味上の主語をつけると，It is important for us to learn to speak English. となる。For us to learn to speak English is important. より形式主語を使った文のほうが自然。

It is quite certain for him to succeed.　彼が成功することは確実だ。

It is not easy for foreign students to live in Japan.

外国人学生が日本で生活するのは容易ではない。

It is very kind of you to say so.　そう言ってくださるとはありがたいことです。

＝You are very kind to say so. と言い換えられる。

It was careless of you to leave your bag on the train.

電車の中にかばんを忘れてくるなんてあなたも不注意ですね。

＝You were careless to leave your bag on the train.

It is～of＋O＋to do…の構文をとれる形容詞には以下のようなものがある。

kind, foolish, clever, considerate, generous, brave, courageous, polite, noble, rude, crazy, absurd など，人の性格・性質を表すような形容詞。

また，形式主語 it は to 不定詞をとるだけでなく，動名詞句や that 節をとることもある。

It is natural that she should look after her baby.（It＝that 節以下）

＝It is natural for her to look after her baby.

　彼女が自分の赤ちゃんの面倒をみるのは当然のことだ。

It is（of）no use crying over spilt milk.（It＝crying over spilt milk）

こぼれたミルクを嘆(なげ)いても無駄なことです。→ 覆水(ふくすい)盆に返らず

It is no good discussing what happened.（It＝discussing what happened）

起こってしまったことをあれこれ言ってもしかたがない。

It は形式主語として使われるだけでなく形式目的語としても使える。

I make it a rule to get up at five every morning.

私は毎朝5時に起きることにしている。← 毎朝5時に起きることをルールにしている。

make＋O＋C（OをCにする），it＝to get up at five every morning

■動作を表す受動態　get＋過去分詞／become＋過去分詞

My finger got trapped in the door.　指がドアにはさまった。

I'm getting depressed.　気分が滅入(めい)ってきた。

Japan is still becoming Americanized.

日本は依然としてアメリカ化されている。

過去分詞が補語的に使われて，受け身の意味がうすれた文として次のようなものがある。

Let's get started.　始めましょう。／出発しましょう。

She got married last year.　彼女は去年結婚した。

theme 17 The Flu

P : Patient　D : Doctor

P : I've had this really bad cold for a week.

D : Have you been taking anything for it?

P : Yes, but it doesn't （　1　） any (a) good.

D : Any fever?

P : Just at night.

D : Did you （　2　） a flu shot this year?

P : No, I didn't.

D : A lot of people （　3　） the flu these days. （　4　） me listen to your breathing. The nurse will （　5　） your temperature.

(Later)

D :（　6　） like the flu. This prescription should （　7　） you get over it.

設問 上の会話文を読んで次の設問に答えなさい。

1 空所（1）～（7）に入る適切な動詞を次の（A）～（G）から１つずつ選びなさい。文頭にくる単語も小文字で書いてあるので注意すること。

（A） help　（B） get　（C） take　（D） do　（E） let

（F） looks　（G） have

2 下線部の単語（a）と同じ用法の good を含む文を次の①～④から１つ選びなさい。

① Smoking does more harm than good.

② He was good and angry.

③ It's good to see you again.

④ He is good at diving.

語句解説

- **flu = influenza**　インフルエンザ，流感（りゅうかん）／**catch flu**　流感にかかる
- **have a bad cold**　ひどい風邪をひいている
  I've had this really bad cold for a week.
  この１週間本当にひどい風邪にかかっています。
- Have you been taking anything for it?
  anything = any medicine, it = that really bad cold, take medicine　薬を飲む
- **it doesn't do any good for me = it does no good for me**　その薬は全然私のためになっていない ➡ **do good for** Ⓐ **= do** Ⓐ **good** = Ⓐ のためになる
- **Any fever? =（Do you have）a fever?**　熱はありますか。
- **get a flu shot**　インフルエンザの予防接種をうける
- **have the flu**　今年流行のインフルエンザにかかっている
- **these days**　この頃／**in those days**　あの頃，当時
- **Let me listen to your breathing.**
  あなたの呼吸を聞かせてください。→ 聴診器をあてさせてください。
- **take one's temperature**　～の体温をはかる
- **look like**　～のように見える
- **prescription**　処方箋（せん）
- **get over**（病気が）治る，（病気などを）克服する
- **help + O + do**　Oが～する手助けをする
  This prescription should help you get over it.
  この処方箋はあなたがこのインフルエンザを克服する手助けをしてくれるはずです。→ この処方箋ならインフルエンザに効くはずです。

解答はp.109

テーマ 17 インフルエンザ

患：患者　医：医者

患：この１週間本当にひどい風邪なんです。

医：なにか薬を飲んでいますか。

患：はい，でも全然効かないんです。

医：熱はどうですか。

患：夜だけです。

医：今年は予防接種はうけましたか。

患：いいえうけていません。

医：多くの人々がこの頃はインフルエンザにかかっています。ちょっと聴診器をあててみます。看護師が体温をはかります。

（しばらくして）

医：インフルエンザのようですね。この処方箋ならよくなるはずです。

解答

1 (1) ― (D)　(2) ― (B)　(3) ― (G)　(4) ― (E)　(5) ― (C)
(6) ― (F)　(7) ― (A)

2 ①

解説

1 (1) do **good**　効く，ためになる ➡ この文では not do any good で「全然効かない」。

(2) get **a flu shot**　インフルエンザの予防注射をうける

(3) have **the flu**　インフルエンザにかかる

(4) let＋㊇＋**do**　㊇に～させる

(5) take **your temperature**　熱をはかる

(6) Looks **like～**　～のように見える

(7) help＋㊇＋**do**　㊇が～するうえで役立つ，㊇が～する手助けをする

2 (a) do＋good の good は「善，ためになること」の意の名詞，do＋O（目的語）あるいは，do＋㊇＋good＝do＋good＋for ㊇「㊇に善をもたらす，㊇のためになる」の形で使う。

① 名たばこは有害無益だ。

② 形彼はかなり怒っている。good and で副 **very** の意味。

③ 形またお会いできてうれしいです。

④ 形彼はダイビングが得意です。

文法 語法

■do A good＝do good for A「Aのためになる」

このgoodは名詞で，doの第4文型（SVO_1O_2）

＝第3文型（SVO_2 for O_1）の使いかたになっている。

That medicine will do you good.＝That medicine will do good for you.

その薬は君のためになるでしょう。→ その薬を飲んだら効きますよ。

■look like「～のようである，～しそうだ」

It looks like rain.＝It looks like it is going to rain.　雨が降りそうだ。

It looks like he will win the election.　彼は当選しそうだ。

You look like you had a terrible dream.　君は怖い夢でも見たようだ。

■let の語法

① ㊅に自由に～させる

Father wouldn't let me go abroad alone.

父は私が1人で海外に行くのを許してくれなかった。

② 一人称，三人称について命令文に用いる

Let me do it.　それをやらせてください。

Please let me know as soon as possible if it will be all right.

それでよいかどうかできるだけ早く知らせてください。

③ let go「離す」，let fall「落とす」，let pass「逃す」

Don't let go the rope.　ロープを離すな。

She has never let pass an opportunity.　彼女は決して機会は逃さなかった。

ことわざから学ぶ文法①

□1日にリンゴ1個で医者いらず

An apple a day keeps the doctor away.

➡ a は「〜につき」の意。keep＋O（目的語）＋C（補語）（OをCの状態に保つ）

「1日にリンゴ1個は医者を遠ざけた状態を保つ」が直訳。

He earns three million yen a year.　彼の年収は300万円です。（**a＝per**）

I'm sorry to have kept you waiting so long.

たいへん長らくお待たせしてすみません。

□良薬は口に苦し

Good medicine tastes bitter to the mouth.

➡ taste＋C（補語）（Cの味がする）

This milk tastes sour.　この牛乳はすっぱい味がする。

The rose smells sweet.　バラはいい香りがする。（smell＋C）

I feel doubtful about what you say.（feel＋C）

君の言うことは疑わしい気がする。

He remained single through his life.（remain＋C）

彼は一生独身のままだった。

theme 18 Dehydration

D : Doctor　P : Patient

D : What seems to be the problem?

P : I don't know. I've had this (a) headache for two days. I (b) aspirin but (1) it doesn't (c) any good.

D : Any other problem?

P : I'm a little dizzy sometimes, (d) after running.

D : You're running these days? In this heat?

P : Well, (2) it's good exercise.

D : What do you do after you run?

P : Relax. Have a beer.

D : That might be your problem. In this heat, (3) it's easy to (e) dehydrated, especially if you're exercising a lot. And (f) is diarrhoetic — (4) it doesn't (g) the fluid you need after running. Water does. You've got to (h) more water in this heat and either (i) running for a few days, or do (5) it when it's (j) — at night, perhaps.

設問 上の会話文を読んで次の設問に答えなさい。

1 下線部 (1) ～ (5) の it がそれぞれなにを表すか書きなさい。

2 空所 (a) ～ (j) に文意からみて適当と思われる語句を下の語群からそれぞれ1つずつ選びなさい。

get	replace	take	do	drink	hold off
terrible	cooler	especially	alcohol		

語句解説

- **dehydration**　脱水症　㊍**dehydrate**　～を脱水させる，乾燥させる
- **What seems to be the problem?**　なにが問題であるように思えますか。
  → どうしましたか。
- **aspirin**　アスピリン
- take aspirin の **take** は（薬などを）飲む，服用する。
- **do good**　役立つ，ためになる
  it doesn't do any good　それは（アスピリンは）全然役に立たない → 効かない
- **dizzy**　㊎めまいがする　㊔**dizziness**　めまい
- **especially**　とくに
- Relax. Have a beer. = I relax and have a beer.
- **get dehydrated**　脱水症状になる
- **diarrhoetic**　㊎下痢の，下痢を引き起こすような
  diarrhea　下痢 = **loose bowels**
- **replace**　～に取って代わる
  He replaced his father as president of the company.
  彼が父親に代わって社長になった。
- **fluid**　水分，液体 ➡ 固体は **solid**，気体は **gas**
- Water does. = Water replaces the fluid you need after running.
  ➡ does は replaces の代わりをする代動詞。
- You've got to drink～ = You have got to drink～
  have got to = **have to** = **must**　～しなければならない
- **either A or B**　AかBかどちらか一方
- **hold off～ing**　～するのを控える，延期する
- **do it when it's cooler** = **go running when it is cooler**
  もっと涼しいときに走りなさい

解答はp.115

テーマ 18 脱水症

医：医者　患：患者

医：どうしましたか。

患：わかりません。2日もこのひどい頭痛がしているのです。アスピリンを服用していますが全然効きません。

医：他になにか問題は。

患：ときどき少しめまいがします。とくに走ったあとで……。

医：この頃走っているんですか。この暑いなかを。

患：いい運動です。

医：走ったあとどうしていますか。

患：リラックスしてビールを飲みます。

医：それが問題かもしれません。この暑さでは脱水症状になりやすくなります。とくにあなたが激しい運動をしていれば……。またビールは下痢の原因になり，走ったあとに必要な水分の補給にはなりません。（補給になるのは）水です。この暑さではもっと多くの水分をとらなければなりません。また，数日走るのを控えるか，涼しくなってから ── 夜に走るとかしなければなりません。

解答

1 (1) aspirin (2) running (3) to get dehydrated (4) alcohol
(5) running

2 (a) terrible (b) take (c) do (d) especially (e) get
(f) alcohol (g) replace (h) drink (i) hold off (j) cooler

解説

1 (1) なにが全然役立たないのかと考える。

(2) なにがいい運動？

(3) It is easy to get～，It is…to～の構文なので to 以下を指す。

(4) なにが必要な水分に取って代わらないのかと考える。

(5) either～or… ～に「数日走るのを控える」とあるから，…部分に「もっと涼しくなってからそれをする」とあれば，当然それは走ること（running）を指す。

2 (a) headache を形容する形容詞は terrible しかない。

(b) アスピリンを飲むの「飲む」は drink ではなくて take。

(c) do＋good の熟語。

(d) めまいがするのはとくに走った直後。

(e) get＋C（補語）ここでは「脱水症状になる」。

(f) diarrhoetic なのは alcohol。

(g) ビールは必要な水分に取って代わることはない。replace。

(h) 水を飲むの「飲む」は drink。

(i) 走るのを控えるは hold off。

(j) もっと涼しくなったら走る，だから cooler。

文法 語法

■either A or B「AかBかどちらか一方」

Either you or I am to go.　君か僕かが行かなければなりません。

動詞はBに合わせる。この文では be＋to 不定詞が（～しなければならない）の意。

be＋to 不定詞

①予定（～することになっている）

We are to have a party this Saturday.

今度の土曜日にパーティーを開く予定です。

②義務・命令（～しなければならない）＝should

You are not to smoke in this room.　この部屋ではたばこは吸えません。

③意思（～する意思がある）…If 節で使われる

If you are to study abroad, you have to study harder.

留学したければ君はもっと勉強しなければなりません。

④可能（～できる）＝can…受身の不定詞で使う

Stars are to be seen at night.　星は夜見ることができる。

⑤運命（～する運命だ）

She was never to see her family again.

彼女は再び家族と会うことはなかった。

■neither A nor B「AもBもどちらも～でない」

Neither you nor I know the answer.　君にも僕にもその答えはわからない。

■both A and B 「AもBも両方とも」

Exercise is good for both body and mind.　運動は心にも身体にもいい。

■get＋過去分詞

get＋過去分詞で動作の受動態を表す。get の代わりに become, grow なども使える。I got tired.「疲れた」I'm tired.「疲れている」と比較。前者は状態の変化，後者は状態。

get married　結婚する，**get drunk**　酔っ払う，**get caught in a shower**　にわか雨に降られる，**get disappointed**　がっかりする，**get delighted**　うれしくなる，**get started**　始める

She grew excited.　彼女はわくわくした。

You'll become used to the broken English spoken by them.

彼らの話すへたくそな英語にじきに慣れますよ。

➡ be used to～ing＝be accustomed to～ing（to do～）「～することに慣れている」。be を get や become にすれば「～することに慣れる」になる。

■他動詞＋～ing

◆動詞の目的語として動名詞のみをとる動詞

mind, enjoy, give up, avoid, finish, escape, practice, stop, deny, admit, miss, postpone＝put off, consider　など。

I enjoyed playing soccer with them.（to play は使えない）

◆不定詞のみを目的語にとる動詞

wish, hope, promise, plan, expect, decide, propose, want, intend, agree　など。

I decided to go abroad.（going は使えない）

◆不定詞でも動名詞でもとれて意味的にもあまり変わらないもの

like, begin, start, continue, cease（やめる）など。

I like to play baseball.＝I like playing baseball.

◆不定詞・動名詞の両方とれるが，意味が違う動詞

try, forget, remember, regret　など。

He tried to open the door.　彼はドアを開けようとした。
（開いたかどうかこの文だけでは不明）

He tried opening the door.　彼は試しにドアを開けてみた。（開いた）

I forgot to write to you.　あなたに手紙を書き忘れた。

I forgot writing to you.　あなたに手紙を書いたことを忘れていた。

She remembered to give him the note.　彼女は彼にメモを渡すことを思い出した。
＝彼女は彼に忘れずにメモを渡した。

She remembered giving him the note.

彼女は彼にそのメモを渡したことを覚えていた。

theme 19 A Bad Cough

D : Doctor　N : Nurse

D : Mr. Simpson has a pretty bad cough. He's (1) smoking. I'd like some chest X-rays.

N : Okay.

D : If they look (2), I'd like him to see Dr. Johnson. That's his specialty. Can you find his number (3) me?

N : (4). I'll get him some information (5) that Smokequitters group, too.

D : (6). I don't think he's going to quit (7) his own. But refrain (8) alarming him about it. I don't want him to read (9) the lines and start (10).

設問 上の会話文の空所（1）～（10）に入る適当な語句を次の（a）～（j）から選びなさい。同じ語句を繰り返し使ってもよいものとする。

(a) on　(b) from　(c) between　(d) for　(e) still
(f) of　(g) sure　(h) panicking　(i) good idea
(j) serious

語句解説

- **cough**　咳，咳をする／**have a bad cough**　ひどい咳をする
- I'd like～は I want～の丁寧な表現。

  ➡ ここは，I'd like him to have some chest X-rays. ともいえる。
- **chest X-rays＝chest pictures**　胸部X線写真
- okay＝OK＝O.K.
- **look serious**　重症に見える
- I'd like him to see Dr. Johnson.＝I want him to see Dr. Johnson.

  him＝Mr. Simpson。患者のことなので，「私はシンプソンさんがジョンソン医師に診てもらうことを望む」が直訳。
- **specialty**　専門
- Sure.「いいとも」の意の快諾(かいだく)表現。

  Can you show me the way to the library? —— Sure.
- **information on～**　～の情報　on＝about
- **Smokequitters group**　タバコをやめたい人たちを一緒に集めて教育啓蒙(けいもう)してやめさせるグループ。**"Giving up smoking" group** ともいう。
- **quit**　やめる＝**stop**
- **on one's own**　自分で，独力で
- **refrain from～ing**　～するのを控える

  Please refrain from smoking.　たばこはご遠慮ください。
- **read between the lines**　行間を読む，言外(げんがい)の意味を読みとる
- **start panicking**　パニックになり始める

  panic　うろたえる，あわてふためく（～ing 形には K を加えることに注意。picnic「ピクニックをする」も K を加えて picnicking となる）

解答はp.121

テーマ 19 ひどい咳

医：医者　看：看護師

医：シンプソンさんはかなり咳がひどいね。それでもタバコは吸っているし…。胸部レントゲンをとりたいんだけど。

看：わかりました。

医：もし手におえなければ，ジョンソン医師に診てもらいたいんだ。彼の専門だからね。彼の電話番号探してくれる。

看：わかりました。例の「禁煙クラブ」についての情報も患者さんにあげておきます。

医：それはいいね。彼が１人でやめられるとは思えないし。でも警告を出すのは控えてください。変に勘ぐられてパニックになってほしくないからね。

解答

(1) − (e)　(2) − (j)　(3) − (d)　(4) − (g)　(5) − (a)
(6) − (i)　(7) − (a)　(8) − (b)　(9) − (c)　(10) − (h)

解説

(1) ひどい咳をしているにもかかわらずまだタバコを吸っている。

(2) 胸部レントゲン写真の結果が思わしくないときジョンソン医師に診てもらいたいということなので serious。

(3) 彼の電話番号を私のために見つけてくれませんか。

(4) いいですよ（快諾（かいだく）表現）＝Sure

(5) 〜に関しての情報 on。

(6) 看護師の申し出に対しそれはいい考えだね。

(7) 自分で，独力で

(8) **refrain from〜ing**　〜を控える

(9) **between the lines**　行間を読む➡「言外の意味を察知する」の意の熟語。

(10) **start〜ing**　〜し始める

医療福祉系の職業②

- □保健師　public health nurse
- □助産師　midwife
- □臨床検査技師　medical and public health laboratory technologist
- □診療放射線技師　radiological technologist

文法 語法

■would like〜／Would you like〜？の構文

I would like this pen.　このペンをください。(would like＝want)

I would like to live in the country.　私は田舎(いなか)に住みたい。

Would you like a drink?　飲み物はいかがですか。

Would you like to come to our party?　パーティーにいらっしゃいませんか。

■名詞＋前置詞　特定の名詞のあとに特定の前置詞がくる。

information on (about)　〜の情報，**key to**　〜の鍵，**lecture on**　〜の講義，**effect on**　〜への効果，**authority on**　〜の権威，**exception to**　〜の例外，**influence on**　〜の影響，**pride in**　〜の誇り

A key to success in life is to work hard.　出世の秘訣はまじめに働くことです。

■I don't think that〜「〜ではないと思います」

I don't think that it'll rain tomorrow.　明日雨は降らないと思う。

この文を日本語につられて，I think that it will not rain tomorrow. としてしまいがちだが，英語的には不自然な英文。否定語は先に出すのが原則。

■want＋㊇＋to do〜「㊇に〜してほしい」

I want you to study English harder.　私は君にもっと英語を勉強して欲しい。

I want to study English harder.　私はもっと英語を勉強したい。

■ask＋㊇＋to do〜「㊇に〜してくれるように頼む」

I asked him to wait till the next day.＝I said to him, "Please wait till tomorrow."

翌日まで待ってくださいと彼に頼んだ。

■tell＋㊇＋to do〜「㊇に〜するように言う」

He told me to get up early the next morning.＝He said to me, "Get up early tomorrow morning."　彼は私に翌朝は早く起きるように言った。

ことわざから学ぶ文法②

□酒は百薬の長

Sake is the best of all medicines.

➡ 最上級＋of ～（～のなかで１番…）

He is the tallest of all the boys.

彼はすべての少年のなかで1番背が高い。

She spoke English（the）best of the four.

4人のなかで彼女は1番上手に英語を話した。

副詞の最上級は the を省略できる。

□覆水盆に返らず

It is no use crying over spilt milk.

こぼれたミルクを嘆いてもしかたがない。

What is done cannot be undone.　1度したことはやりなおしがきかない。

➡ It is no use ～ing（～してもしかたない／無駄だ）

＝It is no good～ing　It は～ing 以下を指す。

＝It is useless to～　It は to 不定詞以下を指す。

What is done の what は先行詞を含む関係代名詞で「なされたこと，やってしまったこと」の意。

undo　動 1度したことを元通りにする

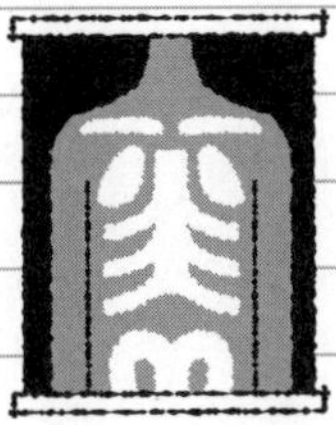

theme 20 Doctor Referral (On the phone)

D1 : Doctor 1　D2 : Doctor 2

D1 : Peter, it's Mark Hodgeman.

D2 : Hi, what's up?

D1 : (1) I've got a patient here I'd like to send your way. Mr. Crane, a 56-year-old white male. History of gastrointestinal problems. An ulcer that won't go away.

D2 : I'm pretty busy these days.

D1 : (2) Couldn't you squeeze him in somehow?
He could be looking at something more serious down the road if he doesn't change his diet for starters.

D2 : Okay. I'll have Karen make an appointment for him. (3) Send me his chart as soon as you can. Has he responded to dietary changes?

D1 : (4) Not as much as I would have liked him to. Maybe you'll have better luck.

設問 上の会話文の下線部（1）～（4）を日本語に訳しなさい。

語句解説

- **referral** （専門医などへの）照会
- **on the phone** 電話で
- **What's up?** どうしたの／なにが起こったのか
  ➡ この表現は挨拶の表現として How are you? と同じように使われることもある。**How are you? Fine.** 元気？ 元気よ／
  What's up? Not much. 変わったことある？ 別にありません。
- I've got a patient～＝I have got a patient～／have got＝have
- **male** 男性の ⇔ **female** 女性の
- **history** 病歴
- **gastrointestinal problems** 胃腸の病気
- **ulcer** 潰瘍（かいよう）／**a stomach ulcer** 胃潰瘍
- **go away** （病気などが）治る
- **these days** この頃 ⇔ **in those days** あの頃，当時
- **squeeze** ～を…のなかに無理やり押し込む
- **somehow** なんとかして
- **down the road**＝**in the future** 将来
- **for starters**＝**to begin with**＝**first of all** まず最初に
- **使役動詞 have＋㊟＋do** ㊟に～してもらう
  I'll have Karen make an appointment for him.
  直訳すると，私はカレンに彼のための予約をしてもらいます。→ カレンに彼の予約を入れるようにしてもらいます。
- **chart**＝**a medical record** カルテ
- **as soon as you can**＝**as soon as possible** できるだけ早く
- **respond to dietary changes** （栄養学的にみた）食事の変更に応じる
- **not as ～as…** …ほど～でない
- **I would have liked him to.**＝**I would have liked him to respond to dietary changes.** 私は彼に食事を変えることに応えてほしかったのですが…。
- **You'll have better luck.** あなたは私よりいい幸運をもつでしょう。
  → あなたのほうが彼に対する治療効果が望めるでしょう。

解答はp.127

テーマ 20 専門医への照会（電話で）

医1：医者1　医2：医者2

医1：ピーターですか。マーク・ホッジマンです。

医2：どうしたの。

医1：あなたのほうへまわしたい患者さんがいるんだけど…。クレーンという名前の56歳になる白人男性です。胃腸の病歴があります。潰瘍が治らないんです。

医2：この頃とても忙しいんだけど。

医1：なんとか予約に入れてもらえませんか。彼はまず食事を変えないと将来ちょっと深刻なことになる可能性があります。

医2：わかりました。カレンに彼の予約を入れさせましょう。できるだけ早くカルテを送ってください。彼は食事を変えることに応じてくれましたか。

医1：こちらが望んだほどは…。たぶんあなたならできると思って。

解答

（1）あなたのほうにまわしたい患者さんがいるんだけど…。
（2）なんとか彼を予約に入れてもらえませんか。
（3）できるだけ早く彼のカルテを私に送ってもらえませんか。
（4）私が彼に望んだほどは（応じてくれていません）。

解説

（1）I've got＝I have got＝I have，here と I'd の間に関係代名詞 whom の省略を理解して訳す。

（2）**squeeze＋(人)＋in**　(人)を（予約に）無理やり押し込む

（3）**send＋O_1＋O_2**　O_1 に O_2 を送る，**as soon as (人) can**　できるだけ～

（4）**not as～as…**　…ほど～でない，**would like to → would have liked to**　～したかったのに… → **would have liked (人) to ～**　(人)に～してほしかったのに
Not as much as I'd have liked him to（respond to dietary changes）
彼に食事を変えることに応えて欲しかったほどには応えてもらえなかった
→ こちらが望んだほどは…

医療福祉系の職業③

□理学療法士	physical therapist，physiotherapist
□作業療法士	occupational therapist
□救急救命士	emergency medical technician，paramedic
□歯科技工士	dental technician

文法 語法

■have got＝have

口語会話ではよく使われる。会話では got だけになる場合もある。

He's got a lot of time on his hands.　彼は暇(ひま)だ。

I've got good news for you.　君にいい話があるよ。

Guess what I've got in my hand.　手の中になにがあるか当ててみて。

I've got to do a lot of homework today.

今日はいっぱい宿題をやらなくてはなりません。

■as～as…「…と同じくらい～」／not as～as…「…ほど～でない」

She is as tall as he.　彼女は彼と同じくらいの背丈です。

She isn't as tall as he.　彼女は彼ほど背が高くありません。

以下のように熟語的に使われる表現もある。

as busy as a bee　とても忙しい

as cunning as a fox　とてもずるい

as like as two peas　うり二つで

as proud as a peacock　とても自尊心の強い

■as～as ㊇ can／as～as possible「できるだけ～，可能な限り～」

He ran as fast as he could.＝He ran as fast as possible.

彼はできるだけ早く走った。

■～times as…as…「…の～倍の…」

This bridge is three times as long as that one.

この橋はあの橋の3倍の長さがある。

He has twice as much money as I do.

彼は私の2倍のお金を持っている。

ことわざから学ぶ文法③

□精神一到何事かならざらん

Where there's a will, there's a way.

will ㊔意志

➡ there's ＝ there is，where は先行詞を含む関係副詞。

「意志があるところに道（方法）がある」が直訳。

Sit where I can see you. 私が見えるところに座ってください。

That's where you're wrong. そこが間違っているところです。

□急がば回れ

The more haste, the less speed.

急いでいるときほどゆっくりやりなさい。

➡ The 比較級～，the 比較級……（～すればするほどますます……）

The more you have, the more you want.

＝**You want the more, the more you have.** 持てば持つほど欲しくなる。

□終わりよければすべてよし

All is well that ends well.

➡ All that ends well is well. と考えればわかりやすい。that は関係代名詞で all が先行詞。バランスよくするために離してある。他に以下のような例もある。

All is not gold that glitters.＝**All that glitters is not gold.**

光るものすべて金とは限らない。

He laughs best who laughs last.＝**He who laughs last laughs best.**

（**he**＝**a man**）

最後に笑う者がもっともよく笑う。

theme 21 A Child's Dentist Appointment

D : Dentist M : Mother

D : Peter's teeth are (1) in good shape, Mrs. Frank. But he's got a lot of overcrowding.

M : Is that a problem?

D : It's actually pretty normal, especially for a growing child. But it (2) does mean braces.

M : I had braces. I hated them.

D : Well, they've changed a lot since we were children. Without them, he'd have more problems later (3) on.

M : Can you recommend someone?

D : Well, Dr. Kelly is someone I've sent a lot of patients (5) to.

M : Where is his office?

D : Not far. A mile or so from here. He's been putting braces (4) on children for twenty years.

M : Braces are awfully expensive, aren't they?

D : They're not cheap, but I think you can work out a payment plan with him.

M : Okay. Do you have his number?

設問 左の会話文の下線部（1）～（5）の単語と同じ用法の文をそれぞれ1つずつ選びなさい。

(1) a. He is <u>in</u> the navy.
b. Mt. Fuji is the highest mountain <u>in</u> Japan.
c. She will come here <u>in</u> an hour.
d. Please write <u>in</u> pencil.
e. Is he <u>in</u> good health?

(2) a. That will <u>do</u>.
b. She <u>does</u>n't feel like drinking tonight.
c. He always <u>does</u> what he wants to do.
d. Who <u>does</u> give a presentation on the new products?
e. Hanako speaks English better than I <u>do</u> English.

(3) (4)
a. Children are playing <u>on</u> the street.
b. I came <u>on</u> my bike.
c. I'll visit you <u>on</u> your birthday.
d. From then <u>on</u> she never trusted him again.
e. The lights in the room were all <u>on</u>.
f. He didn't have his glasses <u>on</u>.

(5) a. I gave some candy <u>to</u> her on Valentine's Day.
b. She tore the letter <u>to</u> pieces.
c. I watched the movie from beginning <u>to</u> end.
d. Please give me the key <u>to</u> the door.
e. <u>To</u> our astonishment, she smiled.

解答はp.133

語句解説

- dentist　歯科医
- appointment　予約
- shape　状態・調子／be in good（bad）shape　調子がいい（悪い）
  I am in good shape.　私は身体の調子がいい。
- actually　実際
- normal　正常な ⇔ abnormal　異常な
- especially　とくに
- braces　歯列矯正（きょうせい）器
- hate＝dislike　～が嫌い
- later　あとで＝later on
- recommend　～を推薦する
  recommend A to B　BにAを推薦する　名 recommendation　推薦
- a mile or so　1マイルかそこら
- awfully　非常に，とても（＝very）
- You can work out a payment plan with him.
  彼と支払い計画を練ってつくる。
  → 彼とお支払いについては相談してください。
  work out　他動詞①＝devise　～を練ってつくる　②＝solve　～を苦労して解く
  　　　　　自動詞①＝(事が）うまくいく　②＝～という結果になる
  Work this problem out by yourself.　1人でこの問題を解きなさい。
  The plan worked out quite well.　その計画はとてもうまくいった。

解答

(1) e (2) d (3) d (4) f (5) a

解説

(1) **be in good shape** 〜がいい状態だ（状態の in）

a. 彼は海軍に入っている。**［所属・従事］** b. 富士山は日本で１番高い山だ。**［場所］** c. 彼女は１時間経ったらここに来ます。**［時間の経過］** d. 鉛筆で書いてください。**［道具］** e. 彼は健康ですか。（in good health ➡ 状態の in）

(2) 強調の助動詞 does。

a. それで結構です。**［「（…で）間に合う」の意の本動詞］** b. 彼女は今夜は飲みたい気分ではない。**［否定文をつくる助動詞］** c. 彼はいつもしたいことをしている。**［本動詞］** d. 誰が新商品に関するプレゼン（口頭発表）をしますか。**［強調の助動詞］** e. 花子は私より英語を上手に話す。**［代動詞］**

(3) **later on** あとで（継続の意味を表す副詞 on）

(4) **put something on** 〜を身につける（所持・着用の意味を表す副詞 on）

a. 子どもたちは通りで遊んでいる。（場所を表す前置詞 on）

b. 私は自転車で来ました。（手段の前置詞 on）

c. 僕は君の誕生日に訪ねるつもりです。（時の前置詞 on）

d. そのときから彼女は彼を2度と信頼しなくなった。（継続の副詞 on）

e. その部屋の明かりは全部ついていた。（スイッチ on ⇔ off の副詞）

f. 彼は眼鏡をかけていなかった。（所持・着用の副詞 on）

put on で注意したいのは，He put his hat on. = He put on his hat. ただし，his hat を it にすると He put it on. としかいえない。

(5) **send $O_1 + O_2$ = send O_1 to O_2** O_1 に O_2 を送る

a. 私はバレンタインデーに彼女にチョコレートをあげた。

give $O_1 + O_2$ = give O_2 to O_1

b. 彼女はその手紙をばらばらに破いた。（to pieces ➡ 状態の to）

c. その映画を最初から最後まで見た。（from〜to…「〜から…まで」➡ 終点の to）

d. そのドアの鍵をください。（the key to〜「〜の鍵」➡ 付加・付属の to）

e. 私たちが驚いたことに彼女は微笑みました。

テーマ 21 子どものために歯科予約を入れる

医：歯科医　母：母親

医：フランクさん，ピーターの歯の状態はいいですよ。でも，歯並びがよくありませんね。

母：問題ですか。

医：実際正常です。とくに伸び盛りの子どもにとっては。でも歯列矯正器をつける必要があります。

母：私もつけたことがあります。大嫌いでした。

医：私たちが子どもの頃に比べたら変わってきています。歯列矯正器をつけないとあとで本当の問題が出てきます。

母：誰か推薦してもらえますか。

医：ケリー医師は私が多くの患者さんを紹介している先生です。

母：彼の病院はどこにありますか。

医：遠くありません。ここから１マイルかそこらです。彼は20年も子どもたちに歯列矯正器をつけてきています。

母：歯列矯正器はとてもお金がかかりますよね。

医：安くはありません。ケリー先生と支払い計画はご相談できると思います。

母：わかりました。彼の電話番号を教えてもらえますか。

文法 語法

■現在完了進行形

過去から現在まで継続している動作を表し，今後も続くことを暗示する。

I have been waiting for two hours and she still hasn't turned up.

2時間も待っているのに，彼女はまだ現れません。

I have been living in Sapporo for ten years.

= I have lived in Sapporo for ten years.　私は札幌に10年住んでいる。

この例のように，現在完了形の継続と現在完了進行形がほぼ同じ意味を表すこともある。

■付加疑問文

基本的には，肯定文に続く付加疑問は否定，否定文に続く付加疑問は肯定，命令文は will you（won't you)?，否定命令文は will you?，Let's～. は shall we? となる。

He is an actor, isn't he?　彼は俳優ですね。

He isn't an actor, is he?　彼は俳優ではないですね。

Mary likes sushi, doesn't she?　メアリーは寿司が好きですよね。

Mary doesn't like sushi, does she?　メアリーは寿司は好きではないですよね。

Let's get started, shall we?　始めましょうよ。

Open the window, will you?（won't you?）窓を開けてくれませんか。

Don't speak loud here, will you?　ここでは大きな声で話さないでくださいね。

■to one's + 感情名詞「人が～したことには」

感情を表す名詞としては，**surprise**（驚き），**delight**（喜び），**joy**（喜び），**disappointment**（失望・落胆（らくたん）），**sorrow**（悲しみ），**grief**（悲しみ），**regret**（後悔），**relief**（安心・安堵（あんど）），**embarrassment**（当惑（とうわく））などがある。

To my great surprise, he has failed in business.

私が驚いたことに彼は事業に失敗した。

To the surprise of the guests, he stood on his head on the stage.

お客が驚いたことに彼は舞台の上で逆立ちした。

theme 22 Sleeping pills

D : Doctor　P : Patient

D : I can prescribe something to help you (1) sleeping. It's (2) strong than the over-the-counter stuff.

P : Is it (3) safety?

D : Sure, but you should avoid alcohol (4) during you're on it.

P : Completely?

D : Well, especially (5) on night. You shouldn't mix the two of them.

P : So when do I (6) drink it?

D : Before bed, if you need to. If (7) you already tired and don't need it, don't take it. But if you (8) get up and can't get back to sleep, take one.

P : Is it addictive?

D : Well, it's best not (9) take it many nights in a row, or you might become dependent (10) of it.

設問 上の会話文の下線部（1）～（10）は誤っている。正しい形に直しなさい。

語句解説

- **sleeping pills**　睡眠薬 ➡ **pill** は丸薬・錠剤
- **prescribe**　薬を処方する／**prescription**　処方箋(せん)
- **something to help you sleep**　あなたが眠る手助けをしてくれるなにか
  → 眠れるようにするなにか
- **over-the-counter**　医師の処方箋不要の（売薬）
- **stuff**　物／**household stuff**　家具／**doctor's stuff**　薬
- **sure**　いいとも，もちろん（快諾(かいだく)するときの表現）
- **avoid**　～を避ける
- **alcohol**　アルコール類／**alcoholism**　アルコール中毒
- **while you're on it**　その薬の服用中は
- **completely**　完全に，まったく
- **you shouldn't mix the two of them.**　この2つを混ぜるべきではない。
  → この薬とアルコールは併用してはいけません。
  ➡ shouldn't は mustn't や ought not to より丁寧な禁止表現。
- **wake up**　目覚める
- medicine には，**tablet**　錠剤，**pill**　丸薬，**capsule**　カプセル，**powder**　粉薬，**liquid medicine**　水薬，がある。
- **addictive**（薬などが）習慣性の，中毒性の　㊔ **addiction**　常用
- **in a row**　続けて
- **become dependent on**　～に依存する

解答はp.139

テーマ 22 睡眠薬

医：医者　患：患者

医：眠れるような薬を処方しましょう。処方箋なしで買える大衆薬より強い薬です。

患：安全ですか。

医：もちろんです。でも服用中はアルコールは避けてください。

患：完全にですか。

医：そうですね。とくに夜は（いけません）。薬とアルコールを併用してはいけません。

患：ではいつ薬は飲めばいいんですか。

医：床につく前に必要ならば飲んでください。もう疲れて必要なければ飲むことはありません。しかし目が覚めて眠りに戻れないときは１錠飲んでください。

患：それは習慣性がありますか。

医：続けて毎晩飲まないほうがいいです。そうでないと依存してしまうことになります。

解答

（1）（to）sleep　（2）stronger　（3）safe　（4）while　（5）at
（6）take　（7）you're／you are　（8）wake　（9）to take
（10）on

解説

(1) **help** Ⓐ + (**to**) **do**　Ⓐが～する手助けをする ➡ 原形動詞か to 不定詞でなければならないので（to）sleep。
(2) than があるので比較級の stronger にする。
(3)「安全ですか?」の意味の文で，Is it～? ～には形容詞がくるので safety ではなくて safe。
(4) you're on it が節なので接続詞の while を使う。during は前置詞。
(5) **at night**　夜に
(6) 薬を飲むの「飲む」は drink ではなくて take。
(7) tired は形容詞なので be 動詞を加えて you're にする。
(8) 目が覚めてまた寝つけないときは薬を飲んでください。
get up　起きる，ベッドから出る／**wake up**　目を覚ます
(9) it's best～の it は形式主語で to 不定詞以下を指すことになるので to take にする。
(10) **become dependent on**　～に依存する
⇔ **become independent of**　～から独立する

文法 語法

■不定詞の形容詞的用法

Something to help you sleep は，to 不定詞以下が something を修飾している。something は後ろから修飾される。

something cold（冷たいもの），**something to drink**（飲むもの），

something cold to drink（なにか冷たい飲みもの）

You need someone to talk with.　君には誰か話し相手が必要だ。

She was the first woman to climb the mountain.

彼女がその山に登った最初の女性だった。

不定詞は他に，名詞的なはたらきや副詞的なはたらきもする。

■不定詞の名詞的用法

To sing karaoke is a lot of fun.　カラオケはとても楽しい。

It is important to study English.（it＝to 以下）英語の勉強は大切だ。

I want to watch a basketball game tonight.

今夜はバスケットの試合を見たいと思います。

My dream is to be a famous writer.　私の夢は有名な作家になることです。

■不定詞の副詞的用法

A Mr. Tanaka came to see you last night.

昨夜，田中さんとかいう方があなたに会いに来ました。（**A Mr. Tanaka**　田中さんという方）**[目的を表す]**

I'm glad to see you.　お会いできてうれしいです。**[gladの原因・理由を表す]**

He must be crazy to go out at midnight.

真夜中に外出するなんて彼もどうかしている。**[crazyの判断根拠を表す]**

ことわざから学ぶ文法④

□明日の百より今日の五十

A bird in the hand is worth two in the bush.

手の中の1羽の鳥はやぶの中の2羽の鳥に値する。

➡ **be worth + O （O の価値がある）**

This book is worth reading again.　この本は再読の価値がある。

＝It is worth while reading（to read）this book again.

It は動名詞あるいは不定詞以下を指す形式主語。

while　名 時間

Stay here for a while.　しばらくここにいなさい。

□人の趣味はわからぬもの（蓼（たで）食う虫も好きずき）

There is no accounting for tastes.

There is no～ing＝It is impossible to～　～するのは不可能だ

account for＝explain　～を説明する　**tastes**　名 好み，嗜好（しこう）

It is impossible to account for tastes. ともいえる。

□よく学びよく遊べ

All work and no play makes Jack a dull boy.

➡ **make＋O（目的語）＋C（補語）（O を C にする）**

All work and no play は主語。直訳は「仕事ばかりで遊ぶ時間がないとジャックをつまらない少年にしてしまう」。

The news made us very happy.

その知らせを聞いて私たちはとてもうれしくなった。

I managed to make myself understood in English.

manage to～　どうにか～できる

私は自分自身を英語で人に理解された状態にどうにかできた。

→ 私の英語はなんとか通じた。／英語でなんとか用を足せた。

theme 23 Depression

D : Doctor　P : Patient

D : Well, Mr. Worth, [(1) どうしましたか]?

P : I don't know. I just…feel…down, these days.

D : You mean tired?

P : No. Well, yes. But just…not interested in…anything these days. Not hungry…. A bit sad, I guess. But [(2) どうしてかわからないのです].

D : Anything wrong at work? Home?

P : Not really. My father died last year, but we sort of expected it. [(3) 彼は長い間がんを患っていました].

D : [(4) いくつか質問させてください].

(Later)

D : I know someone you might want to talk to. There's 'being depressed' and 'clinical depression.' He can help you figure out what the real problem is.

P : Is he a psychiatrist?

D : Yes, he is. And [(5) 彼は私の友達です].

設問 上の会話文中の日本語で書かれている（1）～（5）の箇所を，指定された単語数で英訳しなさい。ただし，短縮形を使えるところは短縮形にすること。

(1) 3語で

(2) 4語で

(3) 8語で

(4) 6語で

(5) 5語で

語句解説

- **depression**　憂鬱（ゆううつ），意気消沈
  I suffer from depression.　鬱（うつ）で悩んでいます。
  動 **depress**　（人を）失望させる，落ち込ませる／**I'm depressed.**　私は憂鬱だ・鬱状態だ。
  The news depressed me.＝I was depressed at the news.
  そのニュースに私はがっかりした。
- **What's the trouble?**　困ったことはなんですか。／どうしました。
- **feel down**　意気が上がらない，気落ちしている
- **these days**　この頃／**in those days**　あの頃，当時
- **a bit**　ちょっと，いくぶん＝**a little bit**
  He is a bit angry.　彼はちょっと怒っている。
- **I guess**　～と思う＝**I suppose**
- **Not really**　いえ，別に ➡ 否定・拒否の表現を和らげる表現。
  Did you enjoy the game?　そのゲーム楽しめた？　**Not really.**　いえ，あまり。
- **we sort of expected it.**　私たちは少しそれを予期していました。
- **He had had cancer for a long time.**　彼は長らくがんを患（わずら）っていました。
- **Let me ask～**　～を質問させてください
- **I know someone（whom）you might want to talk to.**　あなたが話したいかもしれない誰かを知っています。→ あなたが相談していただける方を紹介します。
- **being depressed**　気落ちしていること
- **clinical depression**　病気の鬱状態，鬱病
- **figure out＝make out＝understand**　～を理解する，わかる
- **psychiatrist**　精神科医

解答はp.145

テーマ 23 鬱（うつ）

医：医者　患：患者

医：ところで，ワースさん，今日はどうしました。

患：わからないのです。ただ，この頃，落ち込んでて…。

医：疲れですか。

患：いいえ，うむ～，たぶんそうです。でもこの頃なにに対しても興味がわかないんです。腹もすかないし，少し悲しい気分なのです。でも自分でも理由がわからないのです。

医：仕事でなにか悪いことでも？　家庭はどうですか？

患：別にありません。父が昨年亡くなりましたが，多少は覚悟していました。長い間がんを患っていましたから。

医：いくつか質問させてください。

（しばらくして）

医：相談したほうがよろしいかと思う人を私は知っています。「憂鬱状態」と「鬱病」があります。なにが本当の問題か知る手助けをしてくれます。

患：彼は精神科医ですか。

医：そうです。彼は私の友人です。

解答

（1）what's the problem

（2）I don't know why

（3）He had had cancer for a long time

（4）Let me ask you some questions

（5）he's a friend of mine

解説

(1)「どうしましたか」は医者の決まり文句。3語と指定があるので What's the problem? か What's the matter?

(2) 4語指定なので，I don't know のあとに why をもってくる。

(3) My father died last year. をうけて，died までずっとがんを患っていたのだから，過去完了形で He had had cancer，「長い間」は for a long time。

(4)「～させてください」は Let me ask～。

(5) He is my friend. と単純に考えてしまいそうだが，ふつう「私の友達」という場合は a friend of mine か one of my friends。

医療福祉系の職業④

□歯科衛生士　dental hygienist

□鍼灸師（しんきゅうし）　practitioner of acupuncture and moxibustion

□言語療法士　speech therapist

□音楽療法士　music therapist

文法 語法

■過去完了形（had＋過去分詞）

過去のあるときまでの完了・結果・経験・継続などを表す。

She had already left when I arrived.

私が到着したとき彼女はもう出発していた。

I hadn't seen an elephant before I was fifteen years old.

私は15歳になるまで象を見たことがありませんでした。

My teacher corrected my composition which I had written two days before.

先生は私が2日前に書いておいた作文を直してくれた。

■There is（are）～構文

There is＋単数名詞／There are＋複数名詞が基本。この構文で注意したいのは，不特定の新出の「もの」が「ある，いる」という場合はこの構文が使えるが，特定の既知（きち）の「もの，ひと」が「ある，いる」には使えない。

「母は台所にいます」を There is my mother in the kitchen. というのは間違い。正しくは，My mother is in the kitchen.

ものを列挙して「A，B，C…がある」というときは，There are～. ではなく There is～. が使われる。たとえば，There is a desk, a table, and two chairs in the room.

There is no～ing「～するのは不可能だ」

There is no getting over the fence.（＝It is impossible to get over the fence.）

フェンスを乗り越えるのは不可能だ。

There is no telling what may happen next.

＝It is impossible to tell what may happen next.

次になにが起こるかわからない。

意外な意味をもつ単語①

□swimming 「水泳」以外に 名めまい 形めまいがする

I have a swimming in the head.　めまいがする。

My head is swimming — I think I've got a hangover.

めまいがする。二日酔いだと思う。

□period 「ピリオド・終止符」以外に 名月経

I've got my period.　今生理中です。

□culture 「文化」以外に 名培養(ばいよう)，培養された細菌　cultivate 動培養する

Yogurt is made from active cultures.

ヨーグルトは培養した活性菌でつくられる。

□organ 「オルガン」以外に 名器官・臓器　the organs of digestion = digestive organs 消化器官／internal organs 消化器官

□tissue 「ティッシュペーパー」以外に 名細胞の組織

brain tissue 脳細胞／nervous tissue 神経細胞

□boil 「沸騰(ふっとう)する」以外に 名できもの・腫(は)れ物

I have a painful boil on the calf of my left leg.

左足のふくらはぎにできものができて痛いです。

□pupil 「児童・生徒」以外に 名瞳孔・ひとみ

□colon 「コロン(：)」以外に 名結腸

the large intestine = the lower part of the bowels

大腸 = 腸の下部

theme 24 A Blood Transfusion

D : Doctor　P : Patient

D : Before we operate, I should (a) you that sometimes a lot of blood might have to be replaced with this procedure.

P : (b) does that mean?

D : We might need (c) do a transfusion during or after the operation. But we know you're B positive and we have a large, safe supply of blood (d) hand.

P : Are you sure it's safe? I mean with AIDS and all.

D : We screen the blood very carefully. And it might not happen (e) all. But I wanted to (f) you know.

P : Is the blood checked before you use it?

D : (g). Many times. Our blood supply is indispensable, so we're very thorough with it. Some blood products are used (h) plasma and screening procedures are greatly improved (i) what they were a few years ago.

P : Still, I can't help (j) about it, especially with what happened in Japan.

D : We'll get you some brochures that explain the precautions we take (k) blood.

設問 上の会話文中の空所（a）～（k）に入れるのに最も適切な語を下記のそれぞれの番号に対応した語群の中から選びなさい。

(a)	① tell	② say	③ talk	④ speak
(b)	① what	② when	③ how	④ why
(c)	① in	② on	③ at	④ to
(d)	① in	② on	③ at	④ to
(e)	① in	② after	③ before	④ of
(f)	① make	② have	③ let	④ get

(g) ① Fortunately ② Absolutely ③ Luckily ④ Generally
(h) ① to ② of ③ as ④ into
(i) ① about ② on ③ over ④ during
(j) ① worry ② worrying ③ to worry ④ in worrying
(k) ① to ② with ③ out of ④ in

語句解説

- **blood transfusion**　輸血
- **I should tell you that ～**　あなたに言っておかなければならないんですが…
- **replace**　～を取り替える
- **do a transfusion**　輸血をする
- **(type) B positive**　血液型のB＋
  You're B positive. = Your blood type is B positive.
- **supply**　供給
- **on hand**　手元に，持ち合わせて
- **I mean.**　つまり
- **I mean with AIDS and all.**　エイズその他いろいろなことに対して（安全でしょうか）。
- **and all = and all that**　その他いろいろ
- **screen**　～をふるいにかける，～を選別する
- **after all**　万般（ばんぱん）つくしたあとで
- **I wanted to let you know.**　私はあなたに知らせたかった。
- **absolutely**　その通り（Yes を強めた言いかた）
- **indispensable**　必要不可欠な
- **thorough**　徹底的な
- **plasma**　血しょう（血液成分の1つ）
- **I can't help worrying about it.**　それについて心配しないではいられない。
  cannot help～ing = cannot but 原形　～せざるを得ない
- **brochure**　小冊子，パンフレット
- **precaution**　予防措置／**take precautions**　用心する

解答はp.151

テーマ 24 輸　血

医：医者　患：患者

医：手術の前に言っておきたいのですが，この手術には輸血のための血液がたくさん必要になることがよくあります。

患：それはどういうことですか。

医：手術中あるいは手術後に輸血をする必要があるかもしれないということです。あなたの血液型がBだというのはわかっています。そして手元に安全な十分な量の血液があります。

患：安全でしょうか。エイズとかのことです。

医：とても慎重にその血液は検査しています。そのようなことをいろいろやったあとですからなにか起こるということはないでしょう。ただ，知らせておきたかっただけです。

患：使う前にもその血液はチェックされますか。

医：もちろんです。何回も。私たちの血液供給は不可欠で，それだけに徹底的に検査を行っています。血液製剤は血しょうとして使われているのもあります。また，検査の方法は数年前より大きく改善しています。

患：それでもまだ心配しないではいられません。とくに日本で起きたようなことで…。

医：私たちが血液に対してとるべき予防措置を説明した冊子を差しあげます。

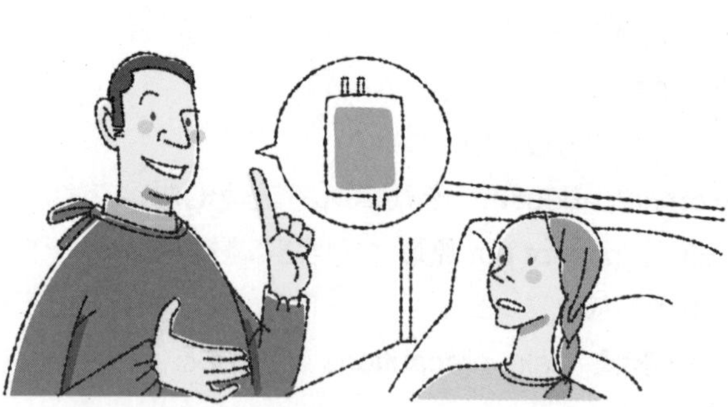

解答

(a) ① (b) ① (c) ④ (d) ② (e) ② (f) ③ (g) ②
(h) ③ (i) ③ (j) ② (k) ②

解説

(a) you と that 節以下が目的語になっている。目的語を 2 つとれるのは tell のみ。
(b) それはどういう意味ですか。➡ mean の目的語なので what。
(c) need to 不定詞
(d) **on hand** 手元に
(e) **after all** いろいろなことをやったあとには…
(f) **let you know** あなたに知らせる／**let me know** 私に知らせてください
(g) もちろんです。その通りです。➡ Yes を強調した表現。
(h) 「～として」の意味の as。
(i) 「～以上に」 血液の安全性の検査は数年前と比べて格段に向上した。
(j) **can't help～ing** ～せざるを得ない，～しないではいられない
(k) 「～に対して」 対象を表す with。

文法 語法

■I mean.「つまり，いやその…」

言い換えたり，言い直したりするときによく会話で使われる表現。

I can do anything for you. I mean, if you want me to do so.

逆に You mean…? となれば,「ということはつまり…」と聞き返しながら確認する表現になる。

■cannot help～ing／cannot but＋原形「～せざるを得ない」(help＝avoid)

I cannot help admitting that I'm wrong.／I cannot but admit that I'm wrong.

私は自分が間違っていると認めざるを得ません。

■replace の語法

◆replace O「O を取り替える」

He replaced the broken window.　彼は割れた窓を取り替えた。

◆replace O_1 with O_2「O_1 をO_2 に取り替える」

I replaced potatoes with sweet potatoes.

私はジャガイモに替えてサツマイモを使った。

◆substitute O_2 for O_1「O_1 をO_2に取り替える」

I substituted sweet potatoes for potatoes.

私はジャガイモに替えてサツマイモを使った。

■supply の語法

㊔供給　**supply and demand**　需要と供給

㊍**supply ㊅ with ㊒ ＝supply ㊒ for ㊅**　㊅に㊒を供給する（不足を補充する）

They supplied the sufferers with food and clothes.

They supplied food and clothes for the sufferers.

彼らは被災者に食糧と衣服を支給した。

provide ㊅ with ㊒ ＝provide ㊒ for ㊅　㊅に㊒を与える

Cows provide us with milk.

Cows provide milk for us.　雌牛は私たちに牛乳を供給してくれる。

意外な意味をもつ単語②

□history 「歴史」以外に 名病歴（= medical history）

He has a history of heart trouble.　彼には心臓病の病歴がある。

Is there any history of cancer in your family?

家系にがんの血統がありますか。

□case 「場合，事例，事件」以外に 名症例，患者

There are twenty cases of measles in this college.

この大学には20名のはしか患者がいる。

□cast 「キャスト，配役」以外に 名ギブス

He's got his leg in a (plaster) cast.　彼は足にギブスをはめている。

□labor 「労働，仕事」以外に 名陣痛，出産の苦しみ

My labor has started.　陣痛が始まりました。

She is in labor now.　彼女は今分娩中です。

□tell 「言う」以外に 動ものをいう，こたえる

Lack of sleep began to tell on him.　睡眠不足が彼にこたえてきた。

□gum 「ゴム，チューインガム」以外に 名歯茎，歯肉

Massage your gums softly after brushing your teeth.

歯を磨いてから軽く歯茎をマッサージしてください。

□last 「最後の」以外に 動続く，もつ

This weather won't last.　この天気はもたないでしょう。

I'm going to stay here as long as my money lasts.

お金が続く限りここにいるつもりです。

theme 25 An Emergency Call

C : Caller

C : Hello! Please help me! My daughter is vomiting blood and can't stop!

911: [(a)]

C : Ten! Ten years old!

911: [(b)]

C : ((1) お腹を押さえて痛いと言っています)

911: [(c)]

C : I don't know!

911: [(d)]

C : No, nothing. My husband took the car, so ((2) 私は彼女を病院に連れて行けません)

911: We can get an ambulance to you. [(e)]

C : Please hurry! …………

911: Don't worry. [(f)]

C : Thank you so much. Bye.

設問 上の会話文を読んで次の設問に答えなさい。

1 空所 (a) ～ (f) に入る適切な文を下の①～⑥から１つずつ選びなさい。

① Any fever?

② Has she ingested anything unusual today?

③ It'll be there in a few minutes.

④ How old is your daughter, ma'am?

⑤ Does she have any other symptoms?

⑥ What's your address and phone number?

2 会話文中の日本語で書かれている箇所 (1) (2) を英語で表現しなさい。

語句解説

- **an emergency call**　緊急電話＝アメリカでは911，日本の119番にあたる。
- **vomit＝throw up**　吐く，もどす
- **ma'am**（一般に女性に対して）奥様
- **symptom**　徴候，症状
- **stomach**　胃，腹
- it hurts ➡ この it は stomach, hurt は自動詞で「～が痛む」。
  My tooth hurts.　歯が痛い。
- **Any fever?＝Do you have a fever?**　熱がありますか。
- **ingest**　飲み込む
- My husband took the car. ➡ この take は「（乗り物に）乗って行く」。
- **～, so……**　～だから……
- **I can't take her to the hospital.**　私は彼女を病院に連れて行けません。
  ➡ この take は「～を…に連れて行く」 take ＋ 人 ＋ to ＋ 場所
- **ambulance**　救急車
- **get**　車などを出す，～を呼ぶ
  We can get an ambulance to you.＝We can get you an ambulance.
  あなたのところに救急車を出すことができます。→ 救急車をまわします。
  I'll get the car.　私が車を出そう。
  Please go（and）get a doctor.　医者を呼んできてください。
- It'll be there in a few minutes. It＝an ambulance
  ➡ in は時間の経過（～経ったら）を表す。be は「いる」。
  I'll be back here in a minute.　すぐに戻ります。

解答はp.157

テーマ 25 緊急電話（911通報）

通：通報者

通　：もしもし！　助けてください。娘が血を吐いて止まらないんです。
911：娘さんは何歳ですか？
通　：10…　10歳です。
911：他になにか症状がありますか。
通　：お腹を押さえて痛いと言っています。
911：熱はありますか。
通　：わかりません。
911：今日，なにか異物を飲み込んでいませんか。
通　：いいえ，なにも。夫が車で出ていますので，病院に連れて行けません。
911：救急車をまわします。住所と電話番号を教えてください。
通　：急いでください。…………
911：ご心配なく。数分で着きますから。
通　：ありがとうございます。では…。

解答

1 (a) ④ (b) ⑤ (c) ① (d) ② (e) ⑥ (f) ③

2 (1) She's holding her stomach and she says it hurts. または
She complains of a pain in her stomach. または
She is crying with her stomach being held. または
She is crying, holding her stomach.

(2) I can't take her to the hospital. または
I can't drive her to the hospital.

解説

1 (a) Ten years old! と答えているので How old〜? の④。

(b)「お腹を押さえて痛いと言っている」のだから，symptoms を訊いているので⑤。

(c) I don't know. に対しては，残りの選択肢のなかでは Any fever? の①がいい。

(d) No, nothing. とあるから異物を飲み込んだか訊いているので②。

(e) 救急車を出すのに住所を訊いているので⑥。

(f) 残りの③，救急車が到着するまで数分だと言っている。

2 (1)「お腹を押さえて」は hold her stomach，「痛い」は hurt。

(2) take＋㊟＋to＋(場所) を使う。

医療福祉系の職業⑤

□あん摩・マッサージ・指圧師　masseur
□臨床心理士　clinical psychologist
□医療秘書　medical secretary
□社会福祉士　certified social worker

文法 語法

■付帯状況の with

With＋O＋C（O が C の状態で，O を C して）

She is lying on the sofa **with her stomach being held.**

お腹を押さえてソファーに横になっています。

with his arms folded　彼は腕を組んで

with my eyes closed　私は目を閉じて

with her mouth full　彼女は口にいっぱいにして，頬(ほお)張って

with the radio on　ラジオをつけたままで

with her legs crossed　彼女は足を組んで

with the engine running　エンジンをかけたままで

Don't speak with your mouth full.　頬張ったままでしゃべるな。

He is sitting on the sofa with his eyes closed.

彼は目を閉じてソファーに座っていた。

■注意したい get の語法

◆get ㊇ to do～「㊇ に～させる」

I got him to help me with my homework.　私は彼に宿題を手伝ってもらった。

What shall I get him to buy me for my birthday?

誕生日に彼になにをねだろうかな？

◆get O done～「O を～される，O を～してもらう」

I must get my PC fixed.　私はパソコンを修理してもらわなければならない。

I got my leg broken in the accident.　私はその事故で足を折った。

◆get O doing～「O を～させる」

He got the engine going.　彼はエンジンを始動させた。

◆have got to do＝got to do＝have to do＝must do「～しなければならない」

I've got to go now.＝I got to go now.　もう行かなければならない。

意外な意味をもつ単語③

□**agree**「同意する」以外に　動（体質）に合う

Fish doesn't agree with me.　魚肉は私の体質に合わない。

□**word**「単語」以外に　名約束，口論

He is a man of his word.　彼は約束を守る男だ。

She had words with him over their kids.

彼女は彼と子どものことで口論をした。

□**head**「頭」以外に　名（コインの）表（⇔ **tails**）

Heads I go, tails you go.　表が出たら僕が，裏なら君が行くんだよ。

□**long**「長い」以外に　動切に願う

They long for peace.　彼らは平和を願っている。

□**short**「短い」以外に　形不足した

We are short of money.　私たちはお金が不足している。

□**business**「ビジネス，職業，仕事」以外に　名干渉する権利，務め

That's none of your business.

＝**That's not your business.**

＝**That's no business of yours.**

＝**Mind your own business.**

それはあなたには関係ないことだ。

theme 26 A Medication Mistake

M : Mother　N : Nurse

(On the phone)

M : Hello! Please help! This is Mrs. Banks!

N : What's the matter, Mrs. Banks?

M : It's my daughter! She's on (1) that medication Dr. George prescribed. But I misread the bottle. I gave her three pills [(a)] one.

N : What medication is that?

M : Amoxicillin. For an earache.

N : Okay. Okay. This has happened before. (2) (need, do, a lot of, give, is, to, her, water, you, what).

M : Water? Just water?

N : That's right. She should be fine. (3) (lots of, water, making, just, her, drink, keep). And don't give her any more medication [(b)] tomorrow.

注：amoxicillin　アモキシシリン（経口ペニシリン）

設問 上の会話文を読んで次の設問に答えなさい。

1 下線部（1）と用法の同じ that を含む文を次の①～④から選びなさい。

① Is she that kind?

② The population of Japan is greater than that of France.

③ This is the same pen that I lost yesterday.

④ Lend me that bike your father bought you for your birthday.

2 下線部（2）（3）の単語を並べ替えて意味の通る文にしなさい。

3 空所（a）（b）に入る適切な語句を下の語群から選びなさい。

（a）because of　owing to　instead of　in spite of　despite

（b）until　by　since　for　during

語句解説

- **This is Mrs. Banks.**　電話で「こちらはバンクスです」。
  ➡ 自分のことでもMrs. Mr. をつけて言うことができる。
- **What's the matter?**　どうしました？
- She's on that medication Dr. George prescribed. は medication のあとに関係代名詞 that が省略されている。that＝the
- **misread**　読み間違える
- **instead of**　～ではなくて，～の代わりに
- **earache**　耳痛／—**ache**　—痛
- Okay＝OK
- what you need to do の what は先行詞の含まれた関係代名詞「あなたがする必要があること」。
- **That's right.**　その通り
- **should**　～のはずだ
- **keep～ing**　～し続ける
- **make＋㊅＋do**　㊅に（無理やり）～させる
- **don't give her any more medication**　彼女にもう薬をあげないでください

解答はp.163

テーマ 26 薬の誤飲

母：母親　看：看護師

（電話で）

母：もしもし，助けてください。バンクスといいます。

看：どうしました，バンクスさん。

母：娘なんです。娘はジョージ先生が処方してくれた薬を使っています。私がビンに書いてある用法を読み間違えたんです。1錠のところを3錠飲ませてしまいました。

看：お薬はなんですか。

母：アモキシシリンです。耳痛用です。

看：それなら大丈夫です，大丈夫。これまでにもありましたから。していただくことは娘さんに水をたくさん飲ませてください。

母：水ですか。水だけでいいんですか。

看：それだけでいいです。大丈夫なはずです。娘さんに水を飲ませ続けてください。そして，明日までは薬は飲ませないでください。

解答

1 ④

2 (2) What you need to do is give her a lot of water

(3) Just keep making her drink lots of water

3 (a) instead of　(b) until

解説

1 ① 彼女はそんなにやさしいの？ ➡「そんなに」の意の副詞。

② 日本の人口はフランスの人口より多い。➡ population の代わりをしている代名詞。

③ これは僕が昨日なくしたペンと同じものだ。

➡ the same～that… 「…と同じ～」(関係代名詞)

④ 君のお父さんが誕生日に買ってくれた自転車を貸してよ。

➡ 関係代名詞の先行詞を強調して the の代わりに使った that。

2 (2) 君がする必要があること＝what you need to do がつくれるかがポイント。

(3) keep～ing と，強制の使役動詞 make＋㊇＋do「㊇に～させる」がポイント。

3 (a) ～ではなくて＝instead of

(b) ～まで＝until

文法 語法

■関係代名詞の先行詞につく that，those

the が強調された that と考えるといい。先行詞が複数形では当然 those になる。

Who was that girl you were talking with?

君が話していた（あの）女の子はだれ？

Those sweets you gave me were very good.

君がくれたキャンディーはとてもおいしかった。

■関係代名詞の what

The boy didn't understand what his teacher said.

その少年は先生が言うことがわからなかった。

Do what is right.　正しいことをしなさい。

Do what you think is right.　君が正しいと思うことをしなさい。

She is quite different from what she was ten years ago.

彼女は10年前の彼女とはまったく違う。

■Keep ～ing＝Keep on ～ing「～し続ける」

The phone kept ringing.　電話が鳴り続けた。

Prices keep on increasing.　物価は上昇し続けている。

It kept raining for a week.　雨が１週間降り続けた。

似た表現に go on～ing がある。

She went on reading.　彼女は読み続けた。

■強制の使役動詞 make，make＋O＋原形動詞「Oに無理やり～させる」

You may take a horse to the water, but you cannot make him drink.

（ことわざ）馬を水場に連れて行くことはできても，水を飲ませることはできない。

What made him do so?＝Why did he do so?

なにが彼をそうさせたか。＝なぜ彼はそうしたのですか。

意外な意味をもつ単語④

□very 「ひじょうに」以外に 形まさにその

This is the very book I've been looking for.

これこそまさに私がさがしていた本です。

□want 「～がほしい，～したいと思う」以外に 名欠乏

She gave up her plan for want of support.

彼女は支援不足で計画をあきらめた。

His nervous breakdown is due to want of sleep.

彼の神経衰弱は睡眠不足からきている。

□hand 「手」以外に 名時計の針，署名，筆跡

the hour［minute］hand 時［分］針

She writes a good hand. 彼女は字がうまい。

□sport 「スポーツ」以外に 名気さくな人，負けっぷりのいい人

He is a good sport. 彼はさっぱりしたいい人だ。

□matter 「物質，問題」以外に 名およその数［量］

a matter of＝about およそ［約］～

in a matter of minutes ものの数分で

□thought 「思考，考え」以外に 名a thought 心もち，少し＝a little

It's a thought too long. それはちょっと長すぎる。

□touch 「～にさわる」以外に 名a touch 少し，ちょっと＝a little

He is a touch naive. 彼はちょっとうぶなところがある。

theme 27 A Skin Problem

N : Nurse　P : Patient　D : Doctor

N : You have a rash?

P : Yes, here on both legs.

N : When did you first notice it?

P : Three days ago. It itches a lot.

N : (A) Is anything bothering you lately at work or at home?

P : No, I'm (a) vacation. Why?

N : Sometimes stress can result (b) hives and produce a rash like that. Did you do any hiking or gardening over the weekend?

P : Yeah, a little yard work.

N : (B) It could be poison ivy. (1) (try, it, scratch, not, do, to). The doctor will be right (c).

(Later)

D : Hmm. It's not so bad, but we'd better take a blood sample and check it (d) allergies or vitamin deficiencies. Do you have any allergies?

P : Well, pollen and cat hair.

D : Ok. Well, we'll know more (e) a couple of days. Meanwhile, please use this cream to relieve any itching.

P : How often should I use it?

D : Whenever it feels itchy. But it washes (f) with water, so don't use it just before showering or bathing. And (2) (keep, to, dry, the skin, try, keeping) in the affected area.

注：poison ivy　うるし

設問 左の会話文を読んで次の設問に答えなさい。

1 空所 (a) ～ (f) に入る適切な前置詞を次の中から選びなさい。同じ前置詞を繰り返し使ってもいいこととする。

from	at	on	in	for	of	above
under	off	down	over	to	with	

2 下線部 (1) を「それをひっかかないようにしてください」，下線部 (2) を「皮膚は乾燥させた状態にしてください」という意味になるように単語を並べ替えなさい。ただし，それぞれ1つ不要な単語を含んでいる。

3 下線部 (A) (B) を，注を参考にして日本語に訳しなさい。

語句解説

- **rash**　発疹
- **itch**　動かゆい　**itchy**　形かゆい
- **bother**　～を悩ます
- **on vacation**　休暇中
- **result in～**　結果として～になる
- **hives**　じんましん
- **gardening**　庭いじり
- **yard work**　庭仕事＝**work in the garden**（英）
- **scratch**　ひっかく
- **we'd better＝we had better**　我々は～したほうがいい
- **take a blood sample**　検査のための血液を採る
- **vitamin deficiencies**　ビタミン欠乏
- **pollen**　花粉
- **meanwhile**　～している間に
- **wash off**　洗い流す
- **affected area**　患部

解答はp.169

テーマ 27 発　疹

看：看護師　患：患者　医：医者

看：発疹ですか。

患：はい，ここです。両足に出ています。

看：最初に気づいたのはいつですか。

患：３日前です。とてもかゆいんです。

看：最近，職場か家庭でなにか悩みごとでもありますか。

患：いいえ，今休暇中なんです。どうしてですか。

看：ときどき，ストレスでじんましんになって，そのような発疹が出ます。週末になにかハイキングか庭いじりをされましたか。

患：はい，ちょっと庭仕事を。

看：うるしかぶれかもしれません。ひっかかないようにしてください。先生が間もなく来ますので。

（しばらくして）

医：えぇ，大したことはありませんが，念のため血液を採ったほうがいいでしょう。そしてアレルギーやビタミン欠乏症を調べるために検査してみましょう。なにか，アレルギーはありますか。

患：花粉と猫の毛です。

医：そうですか。では，２，３日したらもっと詳しいことがわかりますから，その間，この塗り薬をかゆみを和らげるために使ってください。

患：何回くらい使えばいいでしょうか。

医：かゆいときはいつでも。でも，水で洗い流されますのでシャワーやお風呂に入る直前は使わないでください。また，患部は乾燥させておくようにしてください。

解答

1 (a) on　(b) in　(c) in　(d) for　(e) in　(f) off

2 (1) Try not to scratch it

(2) try to keep the skin dry

3 (A) 最近，職場か家庭でなにか悩みごとがありますか。

(B) うるしかぶれかもしれません。

解説

1 (a) on **vacation**　休暇中の

(b) **result** in　結果的に～になる

(c) **The doctor will be right** in**.**　医者がすぐに入ってきます。

(d) for　～のために

(e) in **a couple of days**　2～3日経ったら

(f) **wash** off　洗い流される

2 **try to do～**　～しようとする（試みる）／**try not to do～**　～しないようにする

3 **bother**　～を悩ます，**lately**　最近，**at work**　職場で

文法 語法

■lately と recently「最近，近頃」

主に過去形，現在完了形とともに用いる。

I saw him lately.　私は最近彼に会った。

I received a letter from her recently.　最近彼女から手紙をもらった。

I haven't seen her lately（recently).　最近彼女に会っていない。

「近頃ジムに通っている」は，nowadays か these days を使って，

Nowadays（These days）I go to the gym. といえる。

■result in と result from

Our efforts have resulted in nothing. = Nothing has resulted from our efforts.

我々の努力からはなんの結果も生まれなかった。

result in　～という結果になる

result from　～から結果として生ずる，～に起因する

■try to～「～しようとする」／try～ing「試しに～してみる」

I tried to open the box, but I couldn't.

私はその箱を開けようとしてみたが，できなかった。

I tried opening the box, but there was nothing in it.

私は試しにその箱を開けてみたが中にはなにもなかった。

この 2 つの文からわかるように，箱が開いたのは try ～ing のほう。

try not to～　～しないようにする

Try not to be lazy.　さぼらないようにしてください。

■keep＋O＋C「O を C の状態にしておく」

C には形容詞，現在分詞，過去分詞，前置詞句などがくる。

I kept the window open.　私は窓を開けたままにしておいた。

I'm sorry to have kept you waiting.　お待たせしてすみません。

I kept my book closed.　私は本を閉じたままにしておいた。

It is important to keep ourselves in good health.　健康を保つことが大切です。

英語のなかの IT

あまりに多様に使われるので，重宝ではあるが難しい側面もある。

① 文中の語・句・節を指す

I lost my wallet and I'm looking for it.（it＝my wallet）

He advised me not to smoke, but I thought it very difficult.

（it＝not to smoke）

② とくに指すものはなく，主語の必要性から使われる。天候・時間・明暗などを表したり，特殊構文として使われる

It is ten now.　今10時です。／**It was dark and cold.**　暗くて冷たかった。

It seems that she knows him.　彼女は彼を知っているらしい。

It happened that he went to call on a friend of his.

たまたま彼は友人の1人を訪ねて行った。

It looks very profitable to us.　我々にはとても有益に思われる。

③ 仮主語・仮目的語として使われる

It is important for us to study English.

英語を勉強するのは私たちにとって大切だ。

I think it important for us to study English.

私たちが英語を勉強するのは大切だと私は思う。

I took it for granted that you'd want to go to the movie with us.

当然君も映画を見に行きたいだろうと思ったんだよ。

④ 強調構文（It is ～that…），（It is ～who…），（It is ～which…）

It is I that（who）am to blame.　悪いのは私だ。

It was yesterday that I came across her.

彼女に出会ったのは昨日でした。

⑤ 状況の it…その場の状況で相手がそれとわかること・人・物を表す用法

What makes you so sad?　I just can't help it.

なんでそんなに悲しそうにしてるの？　どうしようもないんだよ。

How is it going with you?　どうですか，お元気ですか？

theme 28 A First Visit

N : Nurse　P : Patient

N : Is this your first (a) to this office?

P : Yes, it is.

N : Okay. Could you take a minute and fill (b) this form? I'll take it when you're (c)?

P : Okay.

N : How will you be (d) for today's visit?

P : Here's my insurance card.

N : How long have you been (e) by this insurance?

P : Two months. It's insurance through my company.

N : Okay. I'm not familiar (f) this insurance plan. Do you have any claim forms with you?

P : No, but (g) the card there's a toll-free number that you can call with questions.

N : Hmm. I'll give them a call. Is this office on your insurance company's list of (h) doctors?

P : Yes. I called them this morning.

N : Good. I'll call them now (i) a claim form. Maybe they can (j) me one.

設問 上の会話文中の空所 (a) ～ (j) に入る適語を下の①～⑩から選びなさい。

① approved　② visit　③ paying　④ covered　⑤ finished
⑥ fax　⑦ with　⑧ out　⑨ on　⑩ about

語句解説・・・・・・・・・・・・・・・・・・・・・・・・・・

- **first visit** 初訪問，初診
- **office** 診療所，クリニック，病院
- **take a minute** 1分時間をとる → ちょっと時間をとる
- **fill out** = **fill in** 〜に必要事項を記入する
- take it の it は this form「用紙をもらいます」。
- **insurance card** 保険証
- **through** 〜を通した，〜による

 insurance through my company 私の会社の保険
- **be familiar with〜** 〜をよく知っている／**be familiar to〜** 〜によく知られている
- **claim form** 保険料の請求用紙
- **toll-free number** フリーダイヤル ➡ アメリカでは an 800 number ともいう。
- **approved doctors** 保険会社から承認された医者（病院）

テーマ 28 初　診

看：看護師　患：患者

看：今回この病院は初めてですか。

患：はいそうです。

看：わかりました。では，ちょっと時間をとっていただきこの書式にご記入いただけますか。終わりましたら取りにまいります。

患：はい。

看：今日はお支払いはどうされますか。

患：ここに保険証があります。

看：どのくらいこの保険に入っていらっしゃるんですか。

患：２か月です。会社の保険です。

看：そうですか。この保険はよくわかりません。保険料請求書をお持ちですか。

患：いいえ，保険証にフリーダイヤルが書かれていますから質問があるときは電話できますよ。

看：電話してみましょう。この病院は保険会社の承認した医者の一覧に入っていますか。

患：はい。今朝電話しました。

看：そうでしたか。保険料請求用紙について今電話して訊いてみましょう。たぶんファックスで１枚送ってくれるでしょう。

解答

(a) ② (b) ⑧ (c) ⑤ (d) ③ (e) ④ (f) ⑦ (g) ⑨
(h) ① (i) ⑩ (j) ⑥

解説

(a) **first** visit　初めて病院に来たこと。visit は名詞。
(b) **fill** out （書式などに）記入する
(c) you are finished「be＋過去分詞」で現在完了形を表す。
finished　完成した，仕上がった
(d) pay **for～**　～に対して支払う
(e) cover は保険でカバーする（まかなわれる）。
(f) **be familiar** with　～をよく知っている
(g) on **the card**　カード（の上）に
(h) approved **doctors**　保険会社の承認（認可）をもらっている医者
(i) about　～について
(j) fax　ファックスを送る

医療福祉系の職業⑥

- □介護福祉士　**care worker**
- □ホームヘルパー　**home helper**
- □介護支援専門員　**care manager**
- □保育士　**child care person, nursery school teacher**

文法 語法

■be＋過去分詞の現在完了形

She is gone.　彼女は行ってしまった。

Spring is come.　春がきた。

このように，往来・発着を表す自動詞は be＋過去分詞で現在完了形をつくることがある。過去分詞が形容詞化して，動作より状態に重きをおいた表現。

■未来進行形（will be～ing）

①確定的な未来の予定

I'll be seeing him soon.　近いうちに彼に会うことになっている。

未来を表す現在進行形の I'm seeing him soon. との違いをみると，現在進行形のほうが比較的近い未来を表すのに対して，未来進行形は比較的遠い未来のことも表せる点で幅が広いといえる。

②未来において進行中の動作を表す

I'll be climbing Mt. Fuji next weekend.

次の週末は富士山を登っていることでしょう。

■未来を表す表現とニュアンスの違い

I leave at six tomorrow.（現在時制）**［他人の意図］**

I'm leaving at six tomorrow.（現在進行形）**［話者・書き手の意図］**

I'm going to leave at six tomorrow.（be going to）**［主語の意図］**

I'm to leave at six tomorrow.（be＋to 不定詞）**［第三者の命令・周囲の事情］**

英語のなかの THAT

① 指示代名詞／指示形容詞

That is Mr. Smith.　あの方はスミスさんです。

That bike is mine.　あの自転車は私のです。

② 副詞

I can't speak that slowly.　そんなにゆっくり話せないよ。

③ 名詞の反復を避けるために用いる

The climate of Japan is milder than that of England.

日本の気候はイギリスより温暖だ。

④ 強調構文

It was on Sunday that I saw him.　私が彼に会ったのは日曜日でした。

It was not until I got home that I missed my bag.

家に着いてはじめてかばんを持っていないことに気づいた。

⑤ 名詞節を導く接続詞として

I think that he will accept my offer.

彼は私の申し出を受け入れてくれると思う。

The truth is that I have never seen her before.

実は私は彼女に会ったことがありません。

You shouldn't forget the fact that smoking is bad for your health.

喫煙は健康によくないということを忘れてはいけません。

⑥ 副詞節を導く接続詞として

I'm surprised that he quit the job.　彼が仕事を辞めたのは驚きだ。

He was so confused that he didn't know what to say.

彼はとても気が動転していてなんて言っていいかわからなかった。

I run fast so that I may catch the train. 私は電車に間に合うように早く走る。

⑦ 関係代名詞

He is the greatest scientist that has ever lived in the world.

彼はこれまでで世界一偉大な科学者である。

theme 29 Weight Gain

D : Doctor　P : Patient

D : Well, now, how can I help you?

P : Well, I've really been (1) on weight lately. At first I thought my wife was (2), but yesterday I couldn't even get a pair of jeans on.

D : Hmm. Have you had any big changes in your lifestyle recently?

P : Well, last March I quit (3) like you told me to.

D : That's often a cause of subsequent weight gain. A lot of people who give up (4) have this problem.

P : Well, what can I do about it?

D : For one thing, exercise. You're (5) to have to start. But also let's talk about your diet.

P : OK. I usually have ham and eggs for breakfast and a cup of coffee with cream. For lunch I eat a hamburger or a hot dog, and for dinner I usually have some kind of meat with potatoes and vegetables.

D : How about dessert?

P : Sometimes I have ice cream or pie.

D : Hmm. Well, you'd better (6) down on the sugar, fat, starch and cholesterol. (a) <u>(three, to, more, a, eggs, It's, have, no, week, than, best)</u>. And have meat (b) twice a day. For dessert, (7) fresh fruit. And substitute pasta (c) potatoes because pasta has more complex carbohydrates.

設問 **左の会話文を読んで次の設問に答えなさい。**

1 空所（1）～（7）に入る適切な動詞を次の語群から選び，文法的に正しい形に変えなさい。同じ動詞を繰り返し使えるものとする。また，形を変えなくてすむものもあるので注意すること。

smoke	cut	kid	have	put	go

2 下線部（a）を「卵は1週間に3個までとするのがベストでしょう」という意味になるように語順を正しなさい。

3 空所（b）に「多くても，せいぜい」の意味の熟語を2語で書きなさい。

4 空所（c）に入る適切な前置詞を書きなさい。

語句解説

- **How can I help you?**　どのようにあなたを手伝えますか。→ どうしましたか。
- **put on weight**　体重が増える，太る ⇔ **lose weight**　やせる
- **at first**　まず最初に
- **kid**　冗談を言う
  No kidding!（自分のことに対して）冗談ではありません，本当です。／（相手の言ったことに対して）冗談でしょう，まさか。
- **get ＋ O ＋ on＝put ＋ O ＋ on**　O を身につける
- **like you told me to**　あなたが私に～するように言ったように（通りに）
- **subsequent**　形 あとに起こる（来る）
- **quit＝give up**　～を止める
- **ham and eggs**　ハムエッグ，**bread and butter**　バターつきのパン
  ➡ 分けないで1つの単語として考える。
- **cream**　クリーム
- **no more than＝only**　～だけ，～しか
- **at most**　多くて，せいぜい
- **substitute A for B**　BをAで取り換える
- **carbohydrate**　炭水化物

解答はp.181

テーマ 29 体重増加

医：医者　患：患者

医：さて，どうしました。

患：えぇ，最近ほんとうに太ってきたんです。最初，妻が冗談を言っていると思っていたんですが，昨日ジーンズがはけなかったんです。

医：ん～。最近なにか生活に大きな変化がありましたか。

患：そうですね…，この3月に先生から言われた通りタバコをやめました。

医：しばしば，タバコをやめるとそのあとに太る原因になります。タバコをやめた人の多くがこの問題に直面します。

患：そうなんですか…。どうしたらいいでしょうか。

医：1つには，運動です。すぐ始めてもらうことになります。ただ，食事療法についても話しましょう。

患：はい。普段朝食にはハムエッグとミルクを入れたコーヒー。昼食にはハンバーガーかホットドッグです。夕食にはたいていなにかの肉とジャガイモそれに野菜を食べます。

医：デザートはどうですか。

患：ときどき，アイスクリームとパイを食べます。

医：そうですか…。糖分，脂肪，でんぷん質，コレステロールは減らしたほうがいいでしょう。卵は1週間に3個までとするのがベストでしょう。また，肉は1日に多くて2回にしてください。デザートには新鮮な果物をとってください。それと，ジャガイモの代わりに麺類をとるようにしてください。麺類のほうが色々な炭水化物を含んでいますから。

解答

1 (1) putting　(2) kidding　(3) smoking　(4) smoking　(5) going
(6) cut　(7) have

2 It's best to have no more than three eggs a week

3 at most

4 for

解説

1 (1) put on weight で「太る」。現在完了進行形なので putting にする。

(2) **kid**　冗談を言う ➡ was があるので過去進行形で kidding，You must be kidding! で「冗談でしょう，まさか」の意。

(3) **quit smoking**　タバコをやめる ➡ quit-quit-quit と無変化。また，quit のあとは動名詞。

(4) **give up smoking**　タバコをやめる ➡ give up のあとも必ず動名詞。

(5) be going to　確定した予定「～することになる」

(6) had better のあとなので原形動詞がくる。**cut down on～**　～を減らす

(7) 命令文なので have「食べる」。

文法 語法

■時制の一致

本文中の I thought my wife was kidding.「妻が冗談を言っていると思いました」をみてみよう。

I think my wife is kidding.「私は妻が冗談を言っていると思います」の文で主節動詞（think）が過去になると従節の動詞（is）も過去になる。

I thought my wife is kidding. といえないように，主節の動詞の時制に合わせて従節の動詞の時制を過去の形にすることを時制の一致という。

時制の一致の例外

We learned that water boils at 100℃.［一般的真理］

水は100度で沸騰すると習った。

He said that Paris is the capital of France.［不変の事実］

パリがフランスの首都だと彼は言った。

時制の一致はまた，話法の転換（直接話法から間接話法への転換）のとき重要になる。

He said to me, "You can use this car."

→ He told me that I could use that car.

彼は私にこの車を使ってもいいよと言った。

I said to her, "Are you afraid of snakes?"

→ I asked her if she was afraid of snakes.

私は彼女にヘビが怖いかどうか尋ねた。

He said to me, "What did you buy for my birthday?"

→ He asked me what I had bought for his birthday.

彼は私が彼の誕生日になにを買ったのかと尋ねた。

I said to John, "Please open the door."

→ I asked John to open the door.

私はジョンにドアを開けてくれるように頼んだ。

英語の12時制

◇基本時制

現在時制（動詞の現在形）	I get up at six every morning. 毎日6時に起きる。
過去時制（動詞の過去形）	I got up at five yesterday.　昨日5時に起きた。
未来時制（will＋原形動詞）	I will get up at six tomorrow.　明日6時に起きる。

◇進行形

現在進行形（am,is,are＋～ing）	I am studying English now. 今英語を勉強している。
過去進行形（was,were＋～ing）	I was studying English then. そのとき英語を勉強していた。
未来進行形（will＋be＋～ing）	I will be studying English now tomorrow. 明日の今頃英語を勉強しているでしょう。

◇完了形

現在完了形（have／has＋P.P.）	I have visited Paris twice. パリを2回訪れたことがある。
過去完了（had＋P.P.）	I had visited Paris twice before I moved to it. パリに引っ越す前に2回訪れたことがあった。
未来完了（will＋have＋P.P.）	I will have visited Paris three times if I visit it this time. 今回パリを訪れると3回行くことになる。

◇完了進行形

現在完了進行形 （have／has＋been＋～ing）	I have been reading the book. ずっとその本を読んでいる。
過去完了進行形 （had＋been＋～ing）	I had been reading the book. ずっとその本を読んでいた。
未来完了進行形 （will＋have＋been＋～ing）	I will have been reading the book. ずっとその本を読んでいることだろう。

theme 30 Maternity

P : Patient　N : Nurse

(On the phone)

P : Hello, this is Mrs. Smith. I'd like to make an appointment to see Dr. Bahn.

N : Okay. (a)

P : Well, a home pregnancy test I did was positive, and (b)

N : Okay, well…let's see…can you come in Thursday at 4:30?

P : Hmm. That might be difficult. (c)

N : Is 8:30 OK?

P : I'm sorry. (d)

N : How about 1:00?

P : (e)

N : OK. We'll see you Friday at one.

P : Thank you. Bye.

(On Friday)

N : Hello, Mrs. Smith. How are you feeling?

P : I have some morning sickness, and I'm very hungry lately.

N : (f) We'll need a urine sample, but first let's weigh you. The scale is over here.

P : (g)

N : That's very common. We can take some blood too, just to be safe, and we have some vitamins that can give you a little strength. (h)

設問 左の会話文中の空所 (a) ～ (h) に入る適切な文を下の中から選びなさい。

① Are there any openings on Friday?
② That's fine.
③ That's to be expected.
④ What would you like to see her about?
⑤ I feel tired a lot too.
⑥ That's not a good time for me.
⑦ The doctor will be in in a minute to measure your abdomen.
⑧ I'd like to be sure.

語句解説

- **maternity**　妊娠
- **make an appointment**　予約する
- **home pregnancy test**　市販の簡易型妊娠チェックテスト
- **positive**　陽性の ⇔ **negative**　陰性の
- **be sure**　確認する
- **openings**　空き
- **How about～?**　～はどうですか？
- **morning sickness**　つわり
- **I'm very hungry lately.** ➡ 「最近とてもお腹がすく」とか「最近気分がすぐれない」のような表現のときは，lately を現在形とともに使える。
- **That's to be expected.**　それは予想されることです。→ それはよくあることです。
- **urine sample**　尿の試料
- **weigh**　体重をはかる
- **scale**　体重計
- **just to be safe**　念のために
- **strength**　力 ➡ strong の名詞形
- **be in**　入ってくる，入室する
- **in a minute**　1分経ったら → ちょっとしたら
- **measure one's abdomen**　～のお腹の大きさをはかる

解答はp.187

テーマ 30 妊娠

患：患者　看：看護師

（電話で）

患：もしもし，こちらはスミスと申します。バーン先生に診てもらうために予約したいんですが…。

看：はい，どういうことで先生に診てもらいたいんですか。

患：自分で妊娠しているかどうかの簡易試験をしたら陽性反応だったので，確認したいのです。

看：わかりました。それでは，えーとー…木曜4時半に来られますか。

患：む…，ちょっと難しいですね。金曜日にどこか空いている時間ありますか。

看：8時半ではどうですか。

患：すみません。都合がつきません。

看：1時ではどうでしょうか。

患：それならいいですね。

看：決まりですね。では金曜1時にお会いしましょう。

患：ありがとうございます。ではそのとき。

（金曜日に）

看：こんにちは，スミスさん。気分はいかがですか。

患：ちょっとつわりがあります。最近とてもお腹がすくんです。

看：よくあることです。尿検査の必要がありますがまず体重をはかりましょう。体重計はこちらです。

患：またとてもだるいんです。

看：それはとてもよくあることです。念のために血液検査もできます。ちょっと力がつくようなビタミン剤もあります。先生がもうすぐ入ってきてお腹の大きさをはかってくれますよ。

解答

(a) ④　(b) ⑧　(c) ①　(d) ⑥　(e) ②　(f) ③　(g) ⑤
(h) ⑦

解説

妊娠の確認のために受診したいということで電話予約する。そして，予約日に病院に行き看護師に問診されている場面だとわかれば難しくないはず。

① 金曜日に空き時間ありますか。
② それはいいですね。
③ それもよくあることです。
④ どういうことで先生に診てもらいたいんですか。
⑤ まだだるいです。
⑥ それはいい時間ではありません。
⑦ 先生がすぐに入ってきてお腹の大きさをはかってくれますよ。
⑧ 確認したいのです。

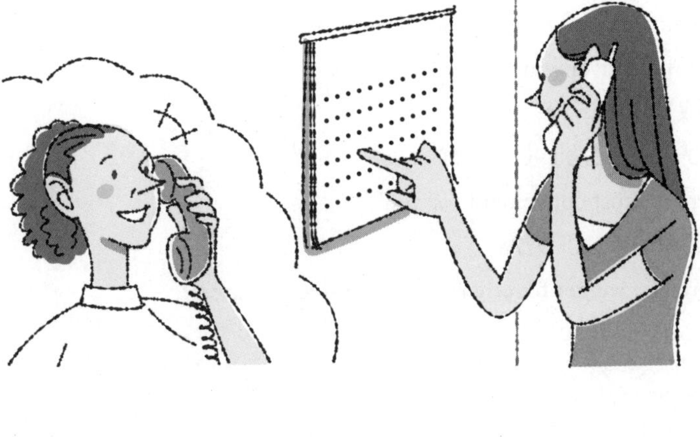

文法 語法

■would like to「～したい」(want to の丁寧表現)

I would like to see Dr. Bahn.　バーン先生に診てもらいたい。

I would like him to study English harder.

彼には今よりもっと英語を勉強してもらいたい。

I would like this book.　この本が欲しいのですが。

Would you like to come with me?　一緒においでになりますか。

Would you like a cup of tea?　紅茶を１杯いかがですか。

I would like to have come to the party.　パーティーに行きたかったのですが。

■時間・場所の取り決め

相手の都合を尋ねる表現

●いつが都合がいいですか。

When will you be available?／When can you make it?／

When would it be convenient for you?

●土曜日の午後は都合がいいですか。

Would Saturday afternoon suit you?／

Would Saturday afternoon be all right with you?

●金曜日の夕方6時はどうですか。

How about Friday evening at six o'clock?

●それで都合がいいですか。

Can you make it?／Will it be all right with you?／

Will it be convenient for you?

場所の取り決め

●どこが１番都合がいいですか。

Where is most convenient for you?

●どこで会いましょうか。

Where can we get together?／Where shall we meet?

実戦入試過去問題

10

1 次の問1～問6の会話の[A]～[F]に入れるのに最も適当なものを，それぞれ下の①～④のうちから1つずつ選べ。 （センター試験改題）

問1

Dr. Ito : How are you today? Is your cold better?

Ms. Smith : A little better, Doctor, but [A]

Dr. Ito : Okay. I'll give you some medicine that will bring it down.

① I don't have a cough anymore. ② I still have a slight fever.

③ I have a runny nose. ④ I'm still feeling a bit weak.

問2

Brian : My family and I moved here last month.

Tomoko : Oh, really? [B]

Brian : Well, it's still pretty new to me, but so far it's great.

① Where are you from? ② How do you like Tokyo?

③ Did you like Tokyo? ④ Why did you move here?

問3

A : Be sure to visit my family while you're in London.

B : I'd love to. In fact, do you think I could stay with them for a couple of days?

A : [C] I'm sure they'd be delighted to have you.

① How come? ② How could you?

③ Why not? ④ Why on earth?

問4

A : What did you think of the movie?

B : [D]

A : Me neither.

① Actually, I didn't really enjoy it. ② To be honest, I hated it.

③ To tell the truth, it wasn't very good. ④ Well, I really loved it.

問5

Jane : I'm sorry, Mom, I broke a lamp in the living room.

Mother : I hope it wasn't the antique that your grandmother gave me.

Jane : [E]

Mother : That's a relief! Grandmother's lamp is our family treasure.

① Luckily, it was. You'll have to buy a new one.

② I'm afraid it wasn't. I like that lamp very much.

③ I'm sorry, it was. And I don't think it can be repaired.

④ No, it wasn't. It was the one you bought last year.

問6

Andy : Would you mind lending me your car tonight?

Yutaka : [F]

Andy : Great! Thank you. I'll bring it back to you tomorrow morning.

① Well, I guess not. ② Of course, I would.

③ Yes, I'd like to. ④ No, I don't think I can.

解答解説は p.203

類題出題大学	東京女子医科大学看護学部看護学科，広島国際大学看護学部看護学科など

2 次のⅠとⅡの対話文を意味の通るように（　）に適語を語群から選びなさい。

（日本赤十字秋田短期大学看護学部）

Ⅰ

Nurse : (　1　) is your problem?

Mr. Johnson : I've had trouble (　2　).

Nurse : (　3　) long have you had this problem?

Mr. Johnson : About a week. It seems to be getting worse day by day.

Nurse : Have you taken any (　4　), Mr. Johnson?

Mr. Johnson : I (　5　) some antihistamines, but it didn't help. I just (　6　) to see if my problem would go away.

注：antihistamines　抗ヒスタミン剤

breathing	what	took	medicine	waited	how

Ⅱ

Nurse : Hi, Mrs. Green … I'm Ms. Mori. Let (　1　) show you around the room.

Mrs. Green : (　2　), thank you.

Nurse : This is (　3　) bed, and this is your bedside table. The nurse call bell is here by the pillow.

Mrs. Green : How does (　4　) work?

Nurse : Just push this button, and the nurse will come to see what you need.

Mrs. Green : Can (　5　) hang my dress?

Nurse : Here's your closet, and that one is for your roommate. Please let me know (　6　) you need anything.

Mrs. Green : O.K., thanks.

I	if	me	it	your	oh

解答解説は p.204

類題出題大学　久留米大学医学部看護学科など

3 問1～問5の対話の空所に入れるのに最も適当なものを，それぞれ下の①～④のうちから1つずつ選べ。 （自治医科大学看護学部）

問1

A : Hi, Susie. How was your date?

B : It was great. The movie was really good. After the movie we went to a restaurant. How was your evening? Did you go to a karaoke club?

A : No, I didn't. I had a headache, so I stayed at home.

B :〔 **1** 〕

① Don't mention it. ② Oh, that's too bad.

③ Sounds great! ④ You're welcome.

問2

A : Hello?

B : Hi, Nicky. This is Pete.

A : Hi, Pete. Er …〔 **2** 〕I'm having dinner.

B : Oh, yes, of course.

① Can I call you back later? ② Can I leave a message?

③ May I speak to Sally? ④ May I ask you a favor?

問3

A : Where did you go on vacation last year, John?

B : Oh, Jenny and I went to Bali.

A : Really?〔 **3** 〕

B : Well, yes, but getting there was pretty stressful. The plane was ten hours late.

① Are you kidding? ② Are you going there again?

③ Did you enjoy it? ④ What's wrong with it?

問4

A : I hear you went to Brazil last summer.

B : That's right.

A :〔　4　〕Is it very different from the U.S.?

B : Yes, it is. Life there seems to be more exciting.

① How far is it?　② What's it like?

③ When did you go?　④ Where were you?

問5

A : What are you looking at, Terry?

B : Oh, just at the movie line-up for next week.

A :〔　5　〕

B : Well, there are some good movies. On Monday afternoon UFO Alert is showing.

① How do you like it?　② I wish I could.

③ What's on?　④ You can't miss it.

解答解説は p.205　類題出題大学　川崎医療福祉大学医療福祉学部・医療技術学部など

4 次の1～5の対話文を読んで，空所に入れるべき適当な英文を（a）～（e）より選びなさい。

（東海大学医療技術短期大学）

1. A : I've gotten a flat tire. I'd like to fix it.
   B : Certainly.（　　　）

2. A : Let's run up to the foot of that hill, shall we?
   B : Yes, let's.（　　　）

3. A : My brother will have an operation next week.
   B : Is that so?（　　　）

4. A : I didn't expect that problem on the exam.
   B : I didn't, either.（　　　）

5. A : I really appreciate your improving my English.
   B : You're welcome.（　　　）

(a) I'll be the first.
(b) Come back in half an hour, please.
(c) I should have prepared better.
(d) I hope it'll be successful.
(e) Tell me when you need me again.

解答解説は p.207

類題出題大学	北里大学医療衛生学部など

5 次の会話は母親とその子供，そして看護師との会話です。空欄（1）～（10）の中に入れるべき適当な語句を選びなさい。（日本赤十字広島看護大学）

Nurse : Good morning. Please come in and (1) a seat here.

Mother : Thank you.

Nurse : And how is your daughter today?

Mother : I'm worried (2) her. She has a sore throat and a fever.

Nurse : (3) has she had the fever?

Mother : I'm not sure. When she came home from school yesterday, she said she had a sore throat. She didn't want to eat dinner and she (4) asleep quite early, about eight o'clock. I took her temperature this morning.

Nurse : (to the child) Does your throat hurt now?

Child : Yes.

Nurse : I'm (5) your temperature now, okay? This won't hurt. First, put this thermometer under your arm, like that. That's it.

Mother : She wanted to go to school this morning. But I thought I should (6) her to the doctor instead of (7) her go to school. She didn't want (8) breakfast because her throat hurt too much.

Nurse : (looking at the thermometer) Yes, you have a fever. Please wait here and the doctor (9) be in to see you in just a minute.

Mother : Oh, thank you. She's usually a healthy child, so I really worry when she (10) feel well enough to eat.

(1) a. sit b. have c. make d. move e. see

(2) a. with b. for c. about d. concerned e. to

(3) a. From when b. When c. To when d. Until when e. How long

(4) a. become b. became c. fell d. is e. got into

(5) a. going to take b. to take c. taking d. will take e. take

(6) a. show b. lead c. make d. take e. bringing

(7) a. forcing b. making c. getting d. letting e. persuading

(8) a. hungry b. any c. a d. no e. to take
(9) a. will b. would c. could d. no word necessary e. soon
(10) a. isn't b. aren't c. doesn't d. wouldn't e. shouldn't

解答解説は p.207 類題出題大学 聖隷クリストファー大学看護学部など

6 次の会話の（1）～（5）内に入れるのに最も適切な表現を下から選びなさい。

（久留米大学医学部看護学科）

A : This small town we've got into is rich in atmosphere.
B : (1) This is certainly different from other places.
A : What is it that makes it look this way, (2)?
B : This is random guess but perhaps all this unique atmosphere comes from its ethnic background.
A : (3) I share your view. (4)! There's a typical folk art souvenir shop over there.
B : (5)! I've long wanted a hand-knit sweater like that.
A : That's what your women's intuition led us to.

(a) Here it is (b) Here I am (c) You said it (d) It sure is
(e) I'm sure. (f) I wonder (g) Look (h) Go ahead

解答解説は p.208 類題出題大学 広島国際大学看護学部看護学科，神戸常盤短期大学看護学科など

7 次の会話の（1）～（5）に入れるのに最も適当な文を，それぞれ下の（a）～（c）のうちから1つずつ選べ。 （川崎医療短期大学）

(N : nurse　P : patient)

N : I'll draw some blood. Please roll up your sleeve.

P : (　1　) I hate this so much.

N : Don't worry. Make a fist like this. Just a little scratch.

P : Ouch! Oh, blood, blood!

N : (　2　) please. That's all. Press here for a few minutes.

P : Is that a thermometer?

N : Yes. (　3　) Keep this until it beeps.

P : OK. Oh, it's beeping.

N : Hmm, 37.5℃. It's a little high. (　4　)

P : No, I don't. But I feel a little tired.

N : How's your appetite?

P : (　5　)

(1) (a) I'm all right.　(b) I'm scared.　(c) I'm fond of shots.

(2) (a) Don't sleep.　(b) Don't move.　(c) Don't take off your shirt.

(3) (a) I took your temperature.　(b) Did you take your temperature?
(c) Let me take your temperature.

(4) (a) Don't you have a headache?　(b) Don't you eat breakfast?
(c) Do you take a bath?

(5) (a) I took plenty of exercise.　(b) I ate all the breakfast.
(c) I slept very well.

解答解説は p.209

類題出題大学　共立女子短期大学看護学科，埼玉医科大学短期大学看護学科など

8 次のA，Bの対話の空所（1）～（6）に，①～④の中から最も適切なものを選んで入れ，対話を完成させなさい。
（北里大学看護学部）

A

Sue : If you ask me, there's too much violence on television. It's made killing seem almost normal.

Doug : （ **1** ）I've never read any proof to support your claim.

Sue : It's common sense. If people keep seeing on TV, they won't care if it happens on their street.

Doug : Maybe, but I've never met anyone who is that apathetic about violence.

Sue : （ **2** ）

Doug : （ **3** ）Take the people on my street. They are not influenced by what happens on television. TV violence doesn't make them more aggressive. Television is just a passive way for them to let off stream.

Sue : Sorry, but I have to disagree.

(1) ① I agree with you on this point.
② Let me try that again.
③ That's just what I was thinking.
④ I'm not sure if I agree.

(2) ① What do you mean?
② But that's impossible!
③ I'll never forget it.
④ I can't do that.

(3) ① I couldn't agree more.
② Can you give me an example?
③ Let me put it another way.
④ Why do you think that?

B

Matt : Oh, I just remembered. Could I use your phone?

Emmy : I'm sorry, (**4**)

Matt : Oh. (**5**) I'll go down to the corner and use the public phone.

Emmy : Do you think you can find your way back?

Matt : (**6**) I know this area like the back of my own hand.

(4) ① but let me get it for you.
② it's out of order.
③ can I get you something?
④ it's all right. I can manage.

(5) ① By the way,
② Since it's just a local call,
③ In that case,
④ Having said that,

(6) ① Is that serious?
② Don't be silly!
③ Where do you mean?
④ Of course not!

解答解説は p.210

類題出題大学 自治医科大学看護学部，駒澤大学医療健康科学部など

9 次の会話文中の空所（A）～（J）に最も適する語句を1～4の中から1つずつ選びなさい。

（東邦大学医学部看護学科）

Henry : I'm going to (A) a little longer tonight.

Bonnie : Do you (B)?

Henry : While I was (C) with a cold, unanswered letters (D).

Bonnie : (E) answer them tomorrow?

Henry : I suppose I can, but I (F).

Bonnie : Your health (G). What (H) more important than that?

Henry : I guess you (I).

Bonnie : Well, (J) till tomorrow what you can't do today. See you tomorrow!

(A) 1. wake up 2. get up 3. take a nap 4. stay up

(B) 1. have to 2. must 3. serious 4. planning to

(C) 1. sickness 2. disease 3. laid up 4. suffer

(D) 1. received 2. piled up 3. were delivered 4. were sent

(E) 1. Don't they 2. Can't you 3. Aren't you 4. Shall you

(F) 1. miss it 2. am bored 3. appreciate it 4. feel guilty

(G) 1. precious 2. worried 3. comes first 4. will be

(H) 1. can be 2. you think 3. do you 4. are you guess

(I) 1. in the wrong reason 2. had better 3. at intervals 4. have a point

(J) 1. take over 2. put off 3. turn down 4. carry out

解答解説は p.211

類題出題大学　埼玉医科大学短期大学看護学科など

10 対話の空所（1）～（5）に入る最も適切な文を（a）～（e）から選びなさい。

（東海大学医療技術短期大学）

Doctor : Please have a seat.

Patient : (　1　)

Doctor : (　2　)

Patient : (　3　)

Doctor : How long have you been experiencing the pain?

Patient : (　4　)

Doctor : (　5　)

Patient : When I bent down to pick up the newspaper.

（a）I've been having a lot of pain in my lower back.

（b）Since Sunday morning —— the day before yesterday.

（c）Now, what seems to be the problem?

（d）When did you first notice the pain?

（e）Thank you.

解答解説は p.212

類題出題大学	東海大学健康科学部看護学科，北里大学看護学部看護学科，呉大学看護学部看護学科など

実戦入試過去問題　解答解説

1　**問1** ②　**問2** ②　**問3** ③　**問4** ①　**問5** ④　**問6** ①

問1 解説

伊藤医師：今日はいかがですか。風邪はよくなりましたか。

スミスさん：ちょっとよくなりましたが，先生，［まだ熱が少しあります］。

伊藤医師：わかりました。熱を下げる薬を出しましょう。

語句　**bring down**　（熱や血圧など）を下げる

問2 解説

ブライアン：家族と僕は先月ここに引っ越してきました。

ともこ：そうですか。［東京はいかがですか］。

ブライアン：えぇ，まだ新しいことばかりで…，でも今のところは順調です。

問3 解説

A：ロンドンにいらっしゃるうちに私の家族を訪ねてくださいね。

B：そうさせてもらいます。実際，２～３日泊めてもらえるでしょうか。

A：［いいですとも］。きっと家族のものも喜びます。

① なぜ？

② How could you（stay with them）？　どうしてできるでしょうか？

③ なぜできないことがありましょうか。→　いいですとも。

④ いったいなぜ？

➡ on earth は疑問詞の強調で，他に in the world, the hell などがある。

問4 解説

A：映画どうだった？

B：［実際，あまり楽しくなかったな］。

A：私もよ。

➡ Me too. ではなくて Me neither. だから否定文をうけて「私も～ではない」という表現。③は否定文ではあるが，主語が it なのでだめ。

➡ “I like sushi.” “Me too.” ／ “I don’t like sushi.” “Me neither.”（口語では Me either. ともいう）

問5 解説

ジェイン：お母さん，ごめんなさい。居間のランプを壊しちゃったの。

母親：おばあちゃんがくれた年代物じゃなければいいけど。
ジェイン：［そうじゃなかったよ。お母さんが去年買ったランプよ］。
母親：安心したわ。おばあちゃんのランプは家の宝だから。
➡ That's a relief.（ほっとした。安心した。）とあるから，骨董物のランプではなかったというのがつかめればいい。

問6 解説

アンディ：今夜君の車貸してくれない？
ゆたか：［うん，いいと思うけど］。
アンディ：うわぁ。ありがとう。明日の朝返すよ。
➡ Would you mind ～ing? のタイプの質問は，mind（気にするか？）と訊いているので，車を貸す場合は「気にしない」と答える。④は「気にしません（貸します），貸せないと思う」とミックスされているのでだめ。

2 **I** (1) What　(2) breathing　(3) How　(4) medicine
(5) took　(6) waited
II (1) me　(2) Oh　(3) your　(4) it　(5) I　(6) if

I 解説

全訳　看：看護師　ジ：ジョンソン
看：どうなさいました。
ジ：息が苦しいんです。
看：いつからですか。
ジ：１週間くらいです。日増しに悪くなっているようなんです。
看：なにか薬を飲みました？
ジ：抗ヒスタミン剤を飲みましたが効きませんでした。ただ，この症状が和らぐのを静観していました。
➡ What is your problem? は「どうしました？」慣用表現。薬を飲むは take。
➡ I've had trouble ～ ing. は have trouble (difficulty) ～ ing「～するのに苦労する，～するのに困難をともなう」という熟語を現在完了形で使ってある。

語句　**wait to see if ～**　～かどうかを静観する，**get worse**　悪くなる，**day by day**　日ごとに・日増しに

Ⅱ 解説

全訳 看：看護師　グ：グリーン

看：こんにちは，グリーンさん。森です。部屋を案内いたしましょう。

グ：ありがとうございます。

看：これがあなたのベッドで，そしてこれがテーブルです。看護師を呼ぶベルは枕のそばのここにあります。

グ：どのように使いますか？

看：このボタンを押すだけです。そうすれば，看護師があなたがなにを必要としているのかを確認しにやってきます。

グ：ドレスを吊るしてもいいですか。

看：ここがあなたのクローゼットで向こうがルームメイトのものです。なにか必要なときは知らせてください。

グ：わかりました。ありがとうございます。

語句 **Let me show you around～** 私にあなたを案内させてください，**使役動詞 let＋㊅＋do，by** ～のそば，**by the pillow** 枕元に，**work** 作動する，**let me know** （私に）知らせる

3 **問1** ②　**問2** ①　**問3** ③　**問4** ②　**問5** ③

問1 解説

A：スージー，デートどうだった？

B：よかったよ。映画ほんとによかった。映画のあとにレストランに行ったのよ。あなたはどうだった？　カラオケに行ったの？

A：行かなかった。頭痛で家にいたのよ。

B：〔 ② それはかわいそうに 〕。

① どういたしまして。　③ すばらしいじゃない。　④ どういたしまして。

➡ ②は同情するときの慣用表現。

➡ ①の Don't mention it. 「もうそれには言及するな」という意味での「どういたしまして」。No problem. という場合もある。

問2 解説

A：もしもし。

B：こんにちは，ニッキー。ピートだよ。

A：こんにちは，ピート。えっと…。〔 ① あとでかけ直していい？ 〕今食事中なの。

B：わかった。

② 伝言いいですか？　③ サリーいますか？　④ お願いがあるんだけど。

➡ ①から③は電話でよく使う慣用表現。

問3 解説

A：ジョン，去年休暇はどこに行ったの？

B：ジェニーと僕でバリに行ったんだ。

A：ほんと。〔 ③ 楽しかった？ 〕

B：ん，まあ，でも着くまでにかなりストレスたまったよ。飛行機が10時間も遅れたんだ。

①冗談でしょ？　② また，そこに行くの？　④ どこか調子悪いの？

➡ ②は現在進行形で未来形を表している。

問4 解説

A：去年の夏ブラジルに行ったそうね？

B：そうだよ。

A：〔 ② どうだった？ 〕アメリカと違った？

B：違ってたね。あそこの生活はエキサイティングだよ。

① どのくらいの距離？　③ いつ行ったの？　④ どこにいたの？

➡ ②の What ～ like? は What is he like?「彼はどんな人ですか」のように様子，風貌（ふうぼう）などを尋ねる慣用表現。

問5 解説

A：テリーなに見てるの？

B：来週の映画欄見てるんだ。

A：〔 ③ なにやってる？ 〕

B：いくつかいい映画あるよ。月曜午後「UFO Alert」があるよ。

① それはどうですか。　② できたらいいな。　④ それは見逃せないよ。

➡ ③は道案内では「必ず見つかります，間違うことはありません」の意味になる。

4　1．(b)　2．(a)　3．(d)　4．(c)　5．(e)

解説

1．A：パンクしました。修理してもらいたいんですけど。
　B：承知しました。(30分後に戻ってきてください)。

2．A：あの丘のふもとまで走ろうよ。
　B：そうしよう。(僕が1番だよ)。

3．A：私の弟は来週手術をうけます。
　B：そうですか。(うまくいけばいいですね)。

4．A：試験であの問題が出るとは思わなかった。
　B：僕もだよ。(もっと準備しとくんだったな)。

➡ should have＋過去分詞「すべきだったのに…（しなかった)」

5．A：私の英語を上達させていただいて本当に感謝しています。
　B：どういたしまして。(また私が必要なときは言ってください)。

5　(1) b　(2) c　(3) e　(4) c　(5) a　(6) d　(7) d　(8) e
(9) a　(10) c

解説

(1) **have (take) a seat**　着席する

(2) **be worried about**　～を心配する

(3) 現在完了なので How long ～？を選ぶ。From when にひっかからないこと。現在完了の継続で起点を表すときは since，期間は for。

(4) **fall asleep**　寝入る

(5) take one's temperature と be going to の組み合わせ。

(6) take＋㊟＋to 場所（㊟を場所に連れて行く）ここでは場所が the doctor 医者のいる所，クリニック，病院のこと。

(7) let＋㊟＋do（㊟に自由に～させる）この文では娘は学校に行きたがっていたので，母親がそれを認めて～させる，～させないという文脈なので let を選ぶ。そして，instead of（～しないで）のあとなので動名詞にする。

(8) **take (have) breakfast**　朝食を食べる　want のあとなので to 不定詞にする。

(9) 命令文＋and ～（…しなさい，そうすれば～）の構文。未来形の will。

(10) worry の時制に合わせて，feel の否定なので doesn't になる。

全訳　看：看護師　母：母親　子：子ども

看：おはようございます。中に入ってここに座ってください。

母：ありがとうございます。

看：娘さん今日はどうしました。

母：心配なんです。のどが痛くて熱もあります。

看：熱はいつからですか。

母：はっきりわかりませんが，昨日学校から帰ってきたときはのどが痛いと言っていました。夕食も食べたがらないでかなり早く8時頃には寝てしまいました。今朝熱をはかりました。

看：（子どもに向かって）今ものど痛い？

子：うん。

看：熱をはかりますね，いいかな。痛くないですよ。まず，この体温計をこのようにわきの下に入れてください。そうです。

母：娘は今朝学校に行くと言いましたが，私は学校に行かせないでお医者さんに診てもらったほうがいいと思いました。のどが痛いから朝食も食べたがりませんでした。

看：（体温計を見ながら）熱がありますね。ちょっとしたらお医者さんが診てくれますからここで待っていてください。

母：ありがとうございます。娘は普段は健康な子なんですよ。だから，体調が悪くて食べられないととても心配なのです。

6　(1) d　(2) f　(3) c　(4) g　(5) b

全訳

A：私たちが着いたこの小さな町は雰囲気がいいね。

B：（ほんと，そうだわね）。他の場所と確かに違うわよね。

A：こんなに見えるのはなん（だろう）？

B：当てずっぽうだけど，この独特の雰囲気は全部少数民族特有の背景からきていると思うわ。

A：（まさにその通りだね）。君の意見に賛成。（見てごらん！）向こうのほうによくある民芸のおみやげ屋さんがあるよ。

B：（着いたわよ）。こんな手編みのセーター欲しかったのよ。

A：女性の直感が導いたってことかな。

表現 **It sure is.** 確かにそうだよね。S is rich in atmosphere. に対して，同意している。

What is it that makes it look this way, I wonder? は強調構文の It is ～ that …で，強調される～のところが疑問詞 what なので上のような語順になっている。I wonder は「～かしら」。I wonder who he is? = Who is he, I wonder? 彼は誰なのかしら？

I share your view. 私はあなたの意見を共有する。→ あなたの意見に賛成する。

Here I am. さあ，着いたよ。**Here it is.** はいどうぞ（物を差し出すとき）。

Go ahead. お先にどうぞ，お話ください，前進などの意。

語句 **get into** ～に着く，**rich** 豊かな・豊富な，**random guess** 当てずっぽう，**ethnic background** （少数）民族特有の背景，**You said it.** その通り，**folk art souvenir shop** 民芸品を扱うおみやげ屋，**over there** 向こうのほう

7 (1) b (2) b (3) c (4) a (5) b

解説

(1) (a) 大丈夫です (b) 怖いです (c) 注射が好きです

(2) (a) 眠るな (b) 動くな (c) シャツを脱ぐな

(3) (a) 体温をはかった (b) 体温をはかりましたか？
(c) 体温をはからせてください

(4) (a) 頭痛がしませんか？ (b) 朝食を食べないの？ (c) 風呂に入る？

(5) (a) 運動をいっぱいしました (b) 朝食を全部食べました
(c) よく眠りました

全訳 看：看護師 患：患者

看：血液を採ります。そでをまくってください。

患：(怖いな)。これって大嫌いなんだ。

看：心配しないでね。このように拳をつくってください。ちょっとチクッとしますよ。

患：痛い。あぁ，血だ。

看：(動かないでください)。もう終わりましたよ。ここを数分押さえてください。

患：それは体温計ですか。

看：そうです。(体温をはからせてください)。ピーッとなるまで押さえてください。

患：はい。あ，鳴ってる。

看：えぇ，37.5℃。ちょっと高いですね。(頭は痛くないですか)。

患：いいえ。でもちょっとだるいです。

看：食欲はどうですか。

患：(朝食は全部食べました)。

8 **A** (1) ④ (2) ① (3) ③ **B** (4) ② (5) ③ (6) ②

A 全訳

スー：言わせてもらえれば，テレビのバイオレンスもの多すぎない。それによって殺人がほとんど普通のことになってしまってるわ。

ダグ：(そうかな？) 君の主張を裏づける証拠について読んだことないよ。

スー：それって常識でしょう。もし銃で撃つのをテレビで見てばかりいたら自分のところで起こっても気にしなくなるわ。

ダグ：たぶん，でもバイオレンスものに対してそんなに冷淡になってる人に僕は会ったことがないよ。

スー：(どういう意味？)

ダグ：(別の言いかたをしようか)。僕の町の人たちのことを取り上げてみよう。彼らはテレビで起こっていることに影響されないし，テレビのバイオレンスものが彼らを攻撃的にすることもないよ。テレビは彼らにとって安全なガス抜き方法なんだよ。

スー：悪いけど，あなたには同意できないわ。

B 全訳

マット：ちょうど思い出した。電話使わせて。

エミー：ごめんなさい。(故障してるの)。

マット：(それなら,) 角まで行って公衆電話を使ってくるよ。

エミー：ちゃんと戻ってこれる？

マット：(ばかなことを言うなよ)。このあたりは自分の庭みたいなところなんだから。

表現 **If you ask me** 言わせてもらうなら・私の意見では，It's made killing

seem almost normal, It's = It has, **make＋O＋do** Oを～させる, **I'm not sure if I agree.** 同意していいものかどうかわからない → そうかな？, **keep ～ing** ～し続ける, **anyone who is that apathetic about violence** バイオレンスものに対してそんなに冷淡な人, **be apathetic about** ～に対して冷淡な, that は apathetic を修飾する副詞「そんなに」, **Let me put it another way.** それを別なもう１つの方法で言わせてください, **know＋O＋like the back of one's hand** O を熟知している

語句 **killing** 殺人, **proof** 証明・証拠, **claim** 主張, **common sense** 常識, **be influenced by** ～に影響をうける, **aggressive** 攻撃的な, **passive** 受身の・受動的な, **let off steam** うっぷんを晴らす・ガス抜きをする, **out of order** 故障中の, **in that case** その状況なら・もしそうなら, **Don't be silly.** 馬鹿を言うな

9 (A) 4　(B) 1　(C) 3　(D) 2　(E) 2　(F) 4　(G) 3
(H) 1　(I) 4　(J) 2

全訳 へ：ヘンリー　ボ：ボニー

へ：今夜ちょっと夜遅くまで起きているつもりなんだ。
ボ：どうしてもなの？
へ：風邪で寝込んでいる間，返事を書いてない手紙がたまってるんだ。
ボ：明日返事を書くってことできないの？
へ：そうしてもいいんだけど，悪いと思って…。
ボ：健康のほうが大事よ。それより大事なものある？
へ：君の言う通りだね。
ボ：「今日できないことは明日に延ばせ」よ。じゃ，またあした。

表現 **stay up** 寝ないで起きている, **be laid up with ～** ～（病気）で寝込む, **You have a point.** 君の言うことにも一理あるね, **You have a good point.** いいところをついてるね, **Go to the point.** ずばり言えよ, Put off till tomorrow what you can't do today. は，ことわざの Don't put off till tomorrow what you can do today.「今日できることを明日に延ばすな」をもじって言ったもの

語句 **put off** 延期する, **take over** ～を引き継ぐ, **turn down** 断る, **carry out** ～を実行する

10 (1) e　(2) c　(3) a　(4) b　(5) d

➡ 典型的な医者と患者の会話なので，流れをきちんとつかめれば楽勝問題。

全訳　医：医者　患：患者

医：座ってください。

患：(ありがとうございます)。

医：(どうなさいました？)

患：(腰がずっと痛いんです)。

医：どのくらいその痛みは続いているんですか？

患：(日曜の朝—おとといからです)。

医：(最初に痛みを感じたのは？)

患：新聞をとろうとして屈(かが)んだときです。

オリジナル問題
完全英文

30

A Cold
A Broken Leg
A Checkup
Chicken Pox
Insomnia
An Allergy
A Urine Test
A Check for Cancer
Blood Pressure
A Change of Hospital Rooms
A Medication Question
Teeth Cleaning
Visiting Hours
A Child Getting a Shot
A Bad Reaction to Medication
AIDS Warning to a Young Patient
The Flu
Dehydration
A Bad Cough
Doctor Referral (On the phone)
A Child's Dentist Appointment
Sleeping pills
Depression
A Blood Transfusion
An Emergency Call
A Medication Mistake
A Skin Problem
A First Visit
Weight Gain
Maternity

theme 1 A Cold

P : Patient D : Doctor Ph : Pharmacist

P : I've had a bad cold for a week.

D : Have you been taking anything for it?

P : Yes, but I don't feel any better.

D : Let's see if you have a fever and I'll listen to your breathing.

(Later)

D : No fever. It's just a cold. This will help you get over it.

P : A prescription?

D : Yes. Have it filled, and take the medicine three times a day after meals.

(At the pharmacist)

Ph : Here you are. Take two capsules after breakfast, lunch and dinner.

P : For how long?

Ph : One week.

P : What if I don't feel better in a week?

Ph : I think you will, but if not, call us and we can refill it for you.

P : Are there any side effects to this?

Ph : Not if you take it as ordered. If you take it on an empty stomach, you might get a little drowsy.

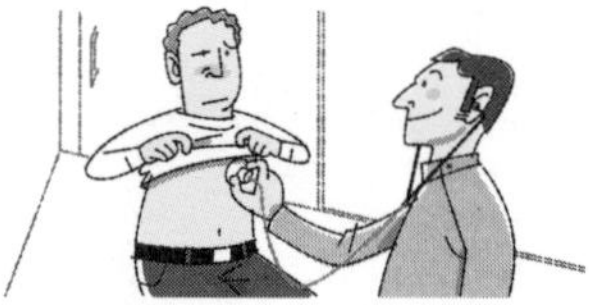

theme 2 A Broken Leg

P : Patient D : Doctor

P : What does the X-ray say?

D : Well, your leg is broken — not too bad, but it's a break. Right here.

P : What do you recommend?

D : We had better put it in a cast — probably for a month.

P : A month?!

D : Bones need time to heal. We can put it in a cast here and give you crutches. It shouldn't take more than an hour.

P : I've never had a cast before.

D : It might take some getting used to, but in order for the bones to mend it's the best thing to do.

P : Are there any restrictions while I have it?

D : Don't get it wet! Also driving a car would be a little dangerous. The key is to keep your weight on the crutches, not your leg.

theme 3 A Checkup

D : Doctor P : Patient

D : What's the problem?

P : Nothing special. I just haven't been here for over a year and thought I ought to have a checkup.

D : How are you feeling?

P : Pretty good. But I've been kind of tired lately.

D : Well, let me listen to your heart and lungs. Are there any changes in your lifestyle? Smoking? Drinking? Diet?

P : No.

D : Hop on the scale. (Later) A few pounds more than last time. What do you do for exercise?

P : I walk during my lunch break almost every day.

D : Compared to doing nothing, that's good, but something that requires more exertion might be in order. Jogging, or cycling ...... something that will bring your heart rate up for 20 or 25 minutes.

theme 4 Chicken Pox

M : Mother N : Nurse

(Mother calls the doctor's office)

M : Hello, my daughter needs to see the doctor.

N : What's the matter, Mrs. ....?

M : Silk. Jane Silk. My daughter, Jane, is one of Dr. Borah's patients. She has spots all over her body.

N : How old is she?

M : She'll be four next month.

N : Do they itch?

M : Yes! She's scratching them all the time.

N : Does she have a fever?

M : A slight one. At night.

N : Sounds like chicken pox. But you'd better bring her in so we can take a look at her.

theme 5 Insomnia

D : Doctor P : Patient

D : So you're having trouble sleeping?

P : Yeah. I get to sleep okay, but then I wake up a few hours later and can't get back to sleep.

D : When did you first notice this?

P : Almost a month ago. I'm tired all day.

D : Are there any big changes in your life? Work? Family?

P : Work is okay. Our new computer system is a nightmare, but everyone feels that way. We're going to have baby in November, but I'm happy about that.

D : Still, a baby and work, that's a lot to think about. Tell me about your exercise, and how much coffee or tea you drink.

P : I jog fifty minutes on Sunday and I drink two cups of coffee a day.

D : When do you drink coffee?

theme 6 An Allergy

P : Patient D : Doctor

P : I think I have a cold. I'm sneezing a lot and my eyes are itchy.

D : Are you coughing?

P : No. I'm just blowing my nose a lot.

D : Do you have any allergies?

P : I don't know. Why?

D : It's spring. A lot of people are allergic to grass or flower pollen, especially in the country. Try DRISTAN — you don't need a prescription for it. If it doesn't work, let us know. We can prescribe something stronger.

P : Are allergies like this serious?

D : Not usually. They're pretty similar to colds, and some people get them every year at this time.

P : But this is the first spring I've ever felt this way.

D : Where did you live before moving here?

P : Chicago.

D : Right in the middle of the city.

P : Yes, downtown.

D : That explains it. In big cities, there usually isn't enough grass or whatever to make it a problem for you. But the first time you're in the country, it really hits you.

theme 7 A Urine Test

N : Nurse　M : Bobby's mother　B : Bobby

N : How is Bobby today?

M : Pretty good. He seems tired a lot but he's pretty busy at school.

N : Good. We'll need a urine sample today. Bobby, can you go to the bathroom for us?

B : But I don't have to go.

N : Well, how about if you have a glass of water and try for us, okay?

M : Come on, Bobby! Drink some water.

N : If you can have him go in this jar, I'll take it when you're done.

M : Exactly what will you test his urine for?

N : We will look for a number of things, such as blood, which could signal an infection, and we'll check the sugar level for diabetes.

theme 8 A Check for Cancer

J : Mrs. Johnson D : Doctor

J : Frankly, I'm a little concerned. I was doing a self exam this Monday and felt what I think was a lump.

D : You're wise to do self exams. Nurse, please come over here. Can you show us where?

J : Here. (Doctor examines her)

D : Hmmm. Your last mammogram was two years ago. Nothing then. We should do another one now to get a better idea.

J : Should I be worried?

D : We'll know more after the mammogram. Tell me about your family. Is there any breast cancer in your family history?

J : My mother hasn't had any problems, but I think my grandmother had a breast removed. Is that important?

D : Yes, it can be. It tends to run in families, but skip generations.

theme 9 Blood Pressure

D : Doctor P : Patient

(At the end of the exam)

D : Your blood pressure is a little high.

P : Is it dangerously high?

D : Any time it's high, it's something to worry about. Your weight doesn't help it. I'd like to see you lose twenty pounds.

P : I hate diets.

D : Well, I'd like you to meet with a nutritionist. She can suggest some changes in what you eat. Rice instead of potatoes, for example.

P : Hmmm.

D : And alcohol. The less, the better.

P : What else?

D : You should cut down on salt and caffeine. Try drinking decaffeinated coffee and juice instead of coke.

P : It sounds like a lot of changes.

D : Yes, but after a while you'll get used to these new foods, and in the long run you'll be better off.

theme 10 A Change of Hospital Rooms

N1 : Nurse 1 N2 : Nurse 2

N1 : Where's Mrs. Benson? I've just been to 401 but she's not there.

N2 : She's been moved.

N1 : When?

N2 : Just a little while ago. Dr. Thomas decided she didn't need to be here.

N1 : Well, I'm supposed to give her a shot at 4 p.m. Where is she?

N2 : 310. But you'd better check her chart. He may have changed the orders.

N1 : I wish someone had told me.

N2 : Dr. Thomas is pretty busy today.

N1 : Are you sure about the room?

N2 : Let's see … yes, 310.

N1 : He never seems to be very considerate of nurses here. He never explains matters or his wishes too well.

N2 : That's true. But if I were in your shoes, I wouldn't complain to anyone. He's pretty well respected around here.

theme 11 A Medication Question

P : Patient Ph : Pharmacist

P : Do you have generic medicine for this prescription?

Ph : Yes, this one costs $15. Just a moment. I'll be back soon.

(Later)

Ph : Here you are. Take it three times a day with meals.

P : Before or after?

Ph : With or after. Take it on an empty stomach and you might feel a little nauseous. Stick to the directions and you'll be fine.

P : Are there any side effects?

Ph : No, but avoid alcohol, or you might get drowsy. If you're on any medication, alcohol is going to affect it, and maybe decrease the effect you want from the medication.

P : Can I get a refill?

Ph : Yes, but you'll need a new prescription.

theme 12 Teeth Cleaning

D.H. : Dental Hygienist P : Patient H : Dr.Hanks

D.H. : How are you today, Mr. Willis?

P : I'm O.K.

D.H. : Just sit back and open wide.

P : Aren't I going to see Dr. Hanks?

D.H. : A little later. First I'll do some cleaning, and then Dr. Hanks will see you.

P : What if I have a cavity?

D.H. : Well, she will talk to you about that, and that's what I'll be looking for.

(Later)

H : It looks like you've got a few cavities, Mr. Willis.

P : Hmm. Well, I'm a little busy today. Can I make an appointment for next week?

theme 13 Visiting Hours

R : Patient's Relative N : Nurse

R : Excuse me, where is Room 401. I'd like to see my aunt.

N : I'm sorry. Visiting hours are from 1:00 to 8:00. It's now eleven thirty. I'm afraid you'll have to wait.

R : But I'd really like to see her.

N : I understand, but those are the rules. If you want to have lunch in the coffee shop, you might be able to see her a little early.

R : But I saw a man go see his wife a minute ago.

N : He's probably a new father. Parents of new babies can come anytime.

theme 14 A Child Getting a Shot

N : Nurse B : Brian M : Mother

N : Hello, Brian. Are you going to be brave today?

B : (silence)

M : He'll try.

B : Why do I have to get a shot?

N : So you won't get sick.

B : Will it hurt?

N : I'll try to be gentle. I don't think it will hurt. Maybe it'll sting for a few seconds, but I bet you'll be brave. Can you roll up your sleeve?

B : But I'm scared.

M : Well, try to be brave and afterwards we'll get some ice cream.

theme 15 A Bad Reaction to Medication

M : Mother N : Nurse

(On the phone)

M : Dr. Harris prescribed an antibiotic for my son's ear infection, but I have a few questions about it.

N : Sure. What would you like to know?

M : He's been taking it for three days, but he doesn't seem any better, and he's very irritable. He won't eat anything.

N : Has he been on this medication before?

M : No, never.

N : It could be an allergic reaction. Some people react that way. Why don't you drop by and the doctor will have another look at him?

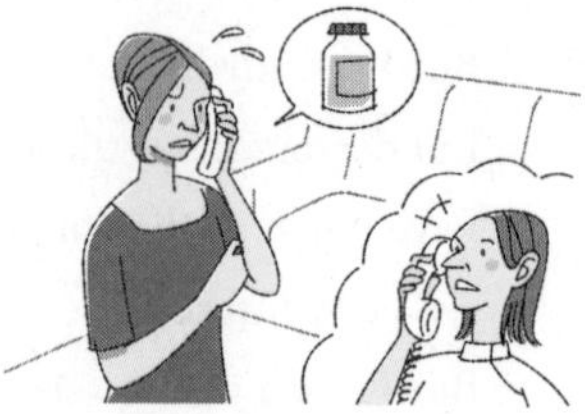

theme 16 AIDS Warning to a Young Patient

D : Doctor P : Patient

D : At your age, it's crucial to understand the risks involved with AIDS.

P : Oh, I know all about that.

D : Good. Still, there are certain things I'd like to remind you of, such as safe sex with a condom, and not using needles or drugs at all, of course.

P : Yeah, I know.

D : Well, a lot of people know these things, but they still get infected.

theme 17 The Flu

P : Patient D : Doctor

P : I've had this really bad cold for a week.

D : Have you been taking anything for it?

P : Yes, but it doesn't do any good.

D : Any fever?

P : Just at night.

D : Did you get a flu shot this year?

P : No, I didn't.

D : A lot of people have the flu these days. Let me listen to your breathing. The nurse will take your temperature.

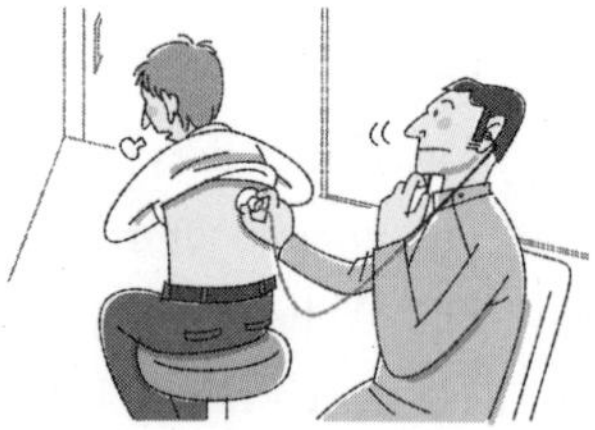

(Later)

D : Looks like the flu. This prescription should help you get over it.

theme 18 Dehydration

D : Doctor P : Patient

D : What seems to be the problem?

P : I don't know. I've had this terrible headache for two days. I take aspirin but it doesn't do any good.

D : Any other problem?

P : I'm a little dizzy sometimes, especially after running.

D : You're running these days? In this heat?

P : Well, it's good exercise.

D : What do you do after you run?

P : Relax. Have a beer.

D : That might be your problem. In this heat, it's easy to get dehydrated, especially if you're exercising a lot. And alcohol is diarrhoetic — it doesn't replace the fluid you need after running. Water does. You've got to drink more water in this heat and either hold off running for a few days, or do it when it's cooler — at night, perhaps.

theme 19 A Bad Cough

D : Doctor N : Nurse

D : Mr. Simpson has a pretty bad cough. He's still smoking. I'd like some chest X-rays.

N : Okay.

D : If they look serious, I'd like him to see Dr. Johnson. That's his specialty. Can you find his number for me?

N : Sure. I'll get him some information on that Smokequitters group, too.

D : Good idea. I don't think he's going to quit on his

own. But refrain from alarming him about it. I don't want him to read between the lines and start panicking.

theme 20 Doctor Referral (On the phone)

D1 : Doctor 1 D2 : Doctor 2

D1 : Peter, it's Mark Hodgeman.

D2 : Hi, what's up?

D1 : I've got a patient here I'd like to send your way. Mr. Crane, a 56-year-old white male. History of gastrointestinal problems. An ulcer that won't go away.

D2 : I'm pretty busy these days.

D1 : Couldn't you squeeze him in somehow?
He could be looking at something more serious down the road if he doesn't change his diet for starters.

D2 : Okay. I'll have Karen make an appointment for him. Send me his chart as soon as you can. Has he responded to dietary changes?

D1 : Not as much as I would have liked him to. Maybe you'll have better luck.

theme 21 A Child's Dentist Appointment

D : Dentist M : Mother

D : Peter's teeth are in good shape, Mrs. Frank. But he's got a lot of overcrowding.

M : Is that a problem?

D : It's actually pretty normal, especially for a growing child. But it does mean braces.

M : I had braces. I hated them.

D : Well, they've changed a lot since we were children.
Without them, he'd have more problems later on.

M : Can you recommend someone?

D : Well, Dr. Kelly is someone I've sent a lot of patients to.

M : Where is his office?

D : Not far. A mile or so from here. He's been putting braces on children for twenty years.

M : Braces are awfully expensive, aren't they?

D : They're not cheap, but I think you can work out a payment plan with him.

M : Okay. Do you have his number?

theme 22 Sleeping pills

D : Doctor P : Patient

D : I can prescribe something to help you sleep. It's stronger than the over-the-counter stuff.

P : Is it safe?

D : Sure, but you should avoid alcohol while you're on it.

P : Completely?

D : Well, especially at night. You shouldn't mix the two of them.

P : So when do I take it?

D : Before bed, if you need to. If you're already tired and don't need it, don't take it. But if you wake up and can't get back to sleep, take one.

P : Is it addictive?

D : Well, it's best not to take it many nights in a row, or you might become dependent on it.

theme 23 Depression

D : Doctor P : Patient

D : Well, Mr. Worth, what's the problem?

P : I don't know. I just … feel … down, these days.

D : You mean tired?

P : No. Well, yes. But just … not interested in … anything these days. Not hungry …. A bit sad, I guess. But I don't know why ….

D : Anything wrong at work? Home?

P : Not really. My father died last year, but we sort of expected it. He had had cancer for a long time.

D : Let me ask you some questions.

(Later)

D : I know someone you might want to talk to. There's 'being depressed' and 'clinical depression.' He can help you figure out what the real problem is.

P : Is he a psychiatrist?

D : Yes, he is. And he's a friend of mine.

theme 24 A Blood Transfusion

D : Doctor P : Patient

D : Before we operate, I should tell you that sometimes a lot of blood might have to be replaced with this procedure.

P : What does that mean?

D : We might need to do a transfusion during or after the operation. But we know you're B positive and we have a large, safe supply of blood on hand.

P : Are you sure it's safe? I mean with AIDS and all.

D : We screen the blood very carefully. And it might not happen after all. But I wanted to let you know.

P : Is the blood checked before you use it?

D : Absolutely. Many times. Our blood supply is indispensable, so we're very thorough with it. Some blood products are used as plasma and screening procedures are greatly improved over what they were a few years ago.

P : Still, I can't help worrying about it, especially with what happened in Japan.

D : We'll get you some brochures that explain the precautions we take with blood.

theme 25 An Emergency Call

C : Caller

C : Hello! Please help me! My daughter is vomiting blood and can't stop!

911 : How old is your daughter, ma'am?

C : Ten! Ten years old!

911 : Does she have any other symptoms?

C : She's holding her stomach and she says it hurts!

911 : Any fever?

C : I don't know!

911 : Has she ingested anything unusual today?

C : No, nothing. My husband took the car, so I can't take her to the hospital.

911 : We can get an ambulance to you. What's your address and phone number?

C : Please hurry! …………

911 : Don't worry. It'll be there in a few minutes.

C : Thank you so much. Bye.

theme 26 A Medication Mistake

M : Mother N : Nurse

(On the phone)

M : Hello! Please help! This is Mrs. Banks!

N : What's the matter, Mrs. Banks?

M : It's my daughter! She's on that medication Dr. George prescribed. But I misread the bottle. I gave her three pills instead of one.

N : What medication is that?

M : Amoxicillin. For an earache.

N : Okay. Okay. This has happened before. What you need to do is give her a lot of water.

M : Water? Just water?

N : That's right. She should be fine. Just keep making

her drink lots of water. And don't give her any more medication until tomorrow.

theme 27 A Skin Problem

N : Nurse P : Patient D : Doctor

N : You have a rash?

P : Yes, here on both legs.

N : When did you first notice it?

P : Three days ago. It itches a lot.

N : Is anything bothering you lately at work or at home?

P : No, I'm on vacation. Why?

N : Sometimes stress can result in hives and produce a rash like that. Did you do any hiking or gardening over the weekend?

P : Yeah, a little yard work.

N : It could be poison ivy. Try not to scratch it. The doctor will be right in.

(Later)

D : Hmm. It's not so bad, but we'd better take a blood sample and check it for allergies or vitamin deficiencies. Do you have any allergies?

P : Well, pollen and cat hair.

D : Ok. Well, we'll know more in a couple of days. Meanwhile, please use this cream to relieve any itching.

P : How often should I use it?

D : Whenever it feels itchy. But it washes off with water, so don't use it just before showering or bathing. And try to keep the skin dry in the affected area.

theme 28 A First Visit

N : Nurse P : Patient

N : Is this your first visit to this office?

P : Yes, it is.

N : Okay. Could you take a minute and fill out this form? I'll take it when you're finished?

P : Okay.

N : How will you be paying for today's visit?

P : Here's my insurance card.

N : How long have you been covered by this insurance?

P : Two months. It's insurance through my company.

N : Okay. I'm not familiar with this insurance plan. Do you have any claim forms with you?

P : No, but on the card there's a toll - free number that you can call with questions.

N : Hmm. I'll give them a call. Is this office on your insurance company's list of approved doctors?

P : Yes. I called them this morning.

N : Good. I'll call them now about a claim form. Maybe they can fax me one.

theme 29 Weight Gain

D : Doctor　P : Patient

D : Well, now, how can I help you?

P : Well, I've really been putting on weight lately. At first I thought my wife was kidding, but yesterday I couldn't even get a pair of jeans on.

D : Hmm. Have you had any big changes in your lifestyle recently?

P : Well, last March I quit smoking like you told me to.

D : That's often a cause of subsequent weight gain. A lot of people who give up smoking have this problem.

P : Well, what can I do about it?

D : For one thing, exercise. You're going to have to start. But also let's talk about your diet.

P : OK. I usually have ham and eggs for breakfast and a cup of coffee with cream. For lunch I eat a hamburger or a hot dog, and for dinner I usually have some kind of meat with potatoes and vegetables.

D : How about dessert?

P : Sometimes I have ice cream or pie.

D : Hmm. Well, you'd better cut down on the sugar, fat, starch and cholesterol. It's best to have no more than three eggs a week. And have meat at most twice a day. For dessert, have fresh fruit. And substitute pasta for potatoes because pasta has more complex carbohydrates.

theme 30 Maternity

P : Patient N : Nurse

(On the phone)

P : Hello, this is Mrs. Smith. I'd like to make an appointment to see Dr. Bahn.

N : Okay. What would you like to see her about?

P : Well, a home pregnancy test I did was positive, and I'd like to be sure.

N : Okay, well … let's see … can you come in Thursday at 4:30?

P : Hmm. That might be difficult. Are there any openings on Friday?

N : Is 8:30 OK?

P : I'm sorry. That's not a good time for me.

N : How about 1:00?

P : That's fine.

N : OK. We'll see you Friday at one.

P : Thank you. Bye.

(On Friday)

N : Hello, Mrs. Smith. How are you feeling?

P : I have some morning sickness, and I'm very hungry lately.

N : That's to be expected. We'll need a urine sample, but first let's weigh you. The scale is over here.

P : I feel tired a lot too.

N : That's very common. We can take some blood too, just to be safe, and we have some vitamins that can give you a little strength. The doctor will be in in a minute to measure your abdomen.

入試直前
チェック!!

医療系によくでる
英単語
370

A

□abdomen 腹部
□abnormal 異常な
⇔ normal 正常な
□abortion 妊娠中絶
□accident 事故
□acute 急性の
⇔ chronic 慢性の
□admission 入院
□aging 老化，加齢
□AIDS
(Acquired Immune Deficiency Syndrome)
エイズ，後天性免疫不全症候群
□allergic アレルギーの
allergic disease アレルギー疾患
□allergist アレルギー専門医
□allergy アレルギー
□ambulance 救急車
□anemia 貧血
□anesthesia 麻酔
□ankle くるぶし
□antibiotic 名形 抗生物質（の）
□appendicitis 虫垂
= appendix
□appetite 食欲
□appointment 予約
□armpit わきの下
□artery 動脈
⇔ vein 静脈
□arthritis 関節炎
□asthma 喘息(ぜんそく)
□attack 発作

B

□back 背中
lower back 腰
backache 腰痛
□bacteria 細菌
□bandage 包帯
□benign 良性の
⇔ malign 悪性の
□birth control 産児制限
□birth rate 出生率
□bleeding 出血
□blood 血液
□blood plasma 血しょう
□blood pressure 血圧
□blood sample 検査用の血液
□blood transfusion 輸血
□blood type 血液型
□blood vessel 血管
□blow nose 鼻をかむ
□body temperature 体温
□boil 煮沸する，できもの・腫れ物
□breast cancer 乳がん
□bruise 打撲傷
□brush 磨く
□burn ～をやけどをする
□burns やけど

C

□calf ふくらはぎ
□cancer cells がん細胞
□cancerous がんの，がんにかかった
□carbohydrate 炭水化物

□carrier 保菌者・保有者
carry 病気を伝える・媒介する
□cast ギプス，～にギプスをする
□cavity 虫歯の穴
□Centigrade ℃，摂氏
□chart カルテ
= a medical record = a clinical record
□check-up 健康診断
□cheek 頬（ほお）
□chest 胸部
□chicken pox みずぼうそう
□chills 寒気
□chin あご先
□cholesterol コレステロール
□chromosome 染色体
□chronic 慢性の
⇔ acute 急性の
□clinical thermometer 体温計
□cold 風邪
□cold medicine 風邪薬
□colon 結腸
□coma 昏睡状態
□complications 併発症，合併症
□congestion 充血
□consult （医者などに）診てもらう
consult a doctor 医者に診てもらう
see a doctorより堅い言いかた
□contact lens コンタクトレンズ
□contagious disease 伝染病
contagious 伝染性の
□cough 咳
□cough drops 咳止めドロップ
□cough medicine 咳止め
□crisis 危機
□crutches 松葉杖
□culture 培養・培養された細菌
cultivate 培養する
□cuts 切り傷

D

□day-care center 託児所，保育園
□death 死
die 動 死ぬ
dead 形 死んだ（状態の）
□death rate 死亡率
□deep breathing 深呼吸
□dehydration 脱水症状
□dental 歯科の
□dental hygienist 歯科衛生士
□dental technician 歯科技工士
□dentist 歯科医
□depression 鬱（うつ）
□diabetes 糖尿病
□diagnose ～と診断する
diagnose her illness as flu
彼女の病気をインフルエンザと診断する
□diagnosis 診断
□diarrhea 下痢
□diet 規定食
be on a diet 食事療法をしている
go on a diet 食事療法をする
□digestion 消化
□discharge 退院
□disinfection 消毒
□doctor’s office 診療所，クリニック
□draw out a teeth 歯を抜く
= put out a teeth
□drip 点滴装置

□drug store 薬局
　= pharmacy

E

□earache 耳の痛み
□egg 卵子
□elbow ひじ
□emergency 緊急事態
□emergency hospital 救急病院
□enzyme 酵素
□epidemic 伝染病の
　an epidemic disease　伝染病
　a cholera epidemic = an epidemic of cholera　コレラの流行
□euthanasia 安楽死
　= mercy killing
□examination 診察
　undergo a medical examination 健康診断を受ける
□eyeball 眼球
□eyebrow 眉毛
□eyedrops 目薬
□eyelashes まつ毛
□eyelid まぶた
□eyesight 視力，視覚
□eye specialist 眼科医
　= oculist
　= ophthalmologist

F

□Fahrenheit 華氏
□failure 不全
　heart failure　心不全
□family dentist かかりつけの歯科医
□family doctor かかりつけの医者
　= family physician
□fat 脂肪
　形 fatty　脂肪の
□feeding problem 消化不良
　= indigestion
□fertilization 受精
□fever 熱
　= temperature
□fill a tooth with cement 歯にセメントを詰める
□fire department 消防署
□first aid 応急手当
□first-aid 応急の
　first-aid kit　救急箱
□first visit 初診
□fit 発作
□flu インフルエンザ
　= influenza
□food poisoning 食中毒
□forefinger 人差し指
□forehead 額
□fracture 骨折

G

□gargle うがい薬，うがいをする
□gene 遺伝子
□general hospital 総合病院
□general practitioner 一般医
　= generalist
□glasses 眼鏡
　= spectacles
□gums 歯茎

H

□harmful 有害な
□hay fever 花粉症
□headache 頭痛
□heal （傷などが）癒(い)える，治る
□health nurse 保健婦
□hearing aid 補聴器
□heart attack 心臓発作
□heart disease 心臓病
□heart failure 心不全
□heel かかと
□hiccup 名 動 しゃっくり（する）
□high blood pressure 高血圧
= hypertension
□high temperature 高熱
□HIV（Human Immunodeficiency Virus） 人免疫欠如ウイルス
□hives じんましん

I

□illness 病気
= sickness
□immune system 免疫系
□immunization 予防接種
□immunology 免疫学
□index finger 人差し指
= forefinger
□indigestion 消化不良
□infection 感染症
airy infection 空気感染
□infectious（epidemic）disease 伝染病，感染症
□inflamed 形 炎症を起こして赤くなった
□influenza インフルエンザ
= flu
□inheritance 遺伝
□in-hospital infection 院内感染
□inject 動 注射する
□injection 注射
= shot
□inpatient 入院患者
⇔ outpatient 外来患者
□insomnia 不眠症
= sleeplessness
□intensive care unit（I.C.U.） 集中治療室
□internal medicine 内科
□internist 内科医
= physician
□intravenous drip 静脈内への滴下注入
□iron 鉄分
□itch 動 かゆい
I itch all over. 体中がかゆい。
□itches 名 かゆみ
□itchy 形 かゆい，むずむずする

J

□jaw あご
□joint 関節
□juice 体液
digestive juice 消化液

K

□kidney 腎臓
□kidney trouble 腎臓障害
□knee ひざ

L

□labor　出産，陣痛
□lack of sleep　睡眠不足
　= want of sleep
□large intestine　大腸
□leukemia　白血病
□life expectancy　平均余命
□life span　寿命
□limb　手足
□lip　唇
□little finger　小指
　= pinky／pinkie
□liver　肝臓
□low blood pressure　低血圧
□lump　しこり
□lung　肺
□lymph　リンパ（液）
□lymphatic　形 リンパの

M

□male nurse　（男性の）看護師
□malignant　形 良性の
　= malign
　⇔ benignant = benign　悪性の
□malnutrition　栄養失調
□malpractice　医療過誤
□mammogram　乳房X線検査
□measles　はしか
□medical attendant　主治医
□medical certificate　診断書
□medical practitioner　開業医
□medication　薬，薬物治療
□mental disorder　精神疾患
□midwife　助産婦
□Ministry of Health, Labor and Welfare　厚生労働省
□misdiagnosis　誤診
□monitor　動 監視する
□morning sickness　つわり
□mumps　おたふくかぜ
□muscle　筋肉
□muscular ache　筋肉痛
□mutant　形 突然変異の

N

□narcotism　麻酔（状態），麻薬中毒
□nasal congestion　鼻づまり
□nausea　吐き気
　形 nauseous　吐き気をもよおす
□navel　へそ
□nearsightedness　近視
□neck　首
□nerve　神経
□neurologist　神経科医
□neurology　神経科
□neurosis　ノイローゼ
□normal　形 正常な
　⇔ abnormal　異常な
□nose　鼻
□nostril　鼻孔
□nurse　看護師，乳母(=nanny)，保母
□nutrition　栄養

O

□obesity　肥満
□ointment　軟膏（なんこう）

□operate 動 ～に手術をする
□operating room 手術室
□operation 名 手術
□organ 器官
　the organs of digestion 消化器官
□outpatient 外来患者
□outpatient department 外来診療所
□over-the-counter 形 医者の処方箋(せん)不要の売薬の，大衆薬の
□overwork 過労
□oxygen 酸素

P

□pacemaker ペースメーカー
□painkiller 痛み止め
　= pain medication
□pain reliever 鎮痛剤
□palm 手のひら
□paralysis 麻痺
□patient 患者
□pediatrician 小児科医
　= children's doctor
□pediatrics 小児科学
□period 月経
□permanent teeth 永久歯
　= adult teeth
　⇔ baby tooth = milk tooth 乳歯
□pharmacy 薬局
□placebo 偽薬
□plague 伝染病，疫病
　（epidemicより猛威をふるうもの）
□pneumonia 肺炎
□poison 毒物
□polio ポリオ，小児麻痺
□pollen 花粉
□positive 形 陽性の
　⇔ negative 陰性の
□pregnancy 名 妊娠
□pregnant 形 妊娠している
□premature 形 未熟な
　⇔ mature 成熟した
□prescription 処方箋
□prevention 予防策（薬）
□private room 個室
□proliferate 動 増殖する
□protein たんぱく質
□psychiatrist 精神科医
□psychiatry 精神科
□psychologist 臨床心理医
□psychology 心理学
□pull out a teeth 歯を抜く
□pulse 脈
　pulse rate 脈拍数
□pupil ひとみ，瞳孔(どうこう)

R

□rash 発疹，湿疹
□rashes かゆみ
□receptionist 受付
□recovery 回復
□red blood cell 赤血球
　⇔ white blood cell 白血球
□rehabilitation 社会復帰，リハビリ
□rest 安静，休息
　take a rest 安静にする，休息をとる
　The doctor ordered her a complete rest. 医者は彼女に絶対安静を命じた。

□ring finger 薬指
□risk 危険性
□rubella 風疹
□runny nose 鼻水

S

□sanatorium 療養所
□scar 傷跡
□senile dementia 老人性痴呆
□sensitive 形 敏感な
⇔ insensitive = dull 鈍感な
□sex 性
□shin すね
□shoulder 肩
□side effects 副作用
□skin disease 皮膚病
□skin irritations かゆみ
□skull 頭蓋骨
□sleeping pill 睡眠薬
□small intestine 小腸
= large intestine 大腸
□sneezing くしゃみ
□sore throat のどの痛み
□specialist 専門医
□spectacles 眼鏡
□sperm 精子
⇔ egg 卵子
□spot 斑点（はんてん）
□stem cell 幹細胞
□stethoscope 聴診器
□stomach 胃，腹
stomachache 胃痛
□stool 便
stool sample 検便用の便
□stress ストレス
□stroke 脳卒中
□stuffy 形 鼻が詰まった
stuffy nose 鼻づまり
□subjective symptom 自覚症状
□sunburn 日焼け
□surgeon 外科医
□surgery 外科
□surgical 形 外科的な
□swimming 名 めまい 形 めまいのする
□symptom 症状

T

□tablet 錠剤
capsule カプセル（薬）
pill 丸薬
□technical expert 技師
□temperature 体温，熱
= fever
□tetanus 破傷風
□therapy 療法
□thermometer 体温計
□thigh 太もも
□thirst 名 渇き
□thirsty 形 のどが渇いた
□throat のど
□thumb 親指
□tissue 細胞の組織
brain tissue 脳細胞
□toenail 足指のつめ
□tongue 舌
□toothbrush 歯ブラシ
□tooth decay 虫歯
= cavity

□toothpaste 練り歯磨き
□transplant 移植する
heart transplant 心臓移植
□treatment 治療
receive medical treatment 医療を受ける
□tuberculosis 結核
□twins 双生児

U

□ulcers 胃潰瘍（かいよう）
□unconscious 形 意識不明の
□unconsciousness 名 意識不明
□upper lid 上まぶた
a double-edged eyelid 二重まぶた
a single-edged eyelid 一重まぶた
□urine 尿
□urine specimen 検尿用の尿

V

□vaccination ワクチン注射
□vaccine ワクチン
□vein 静脈
⇔ artery 動脈
□virus ウイルス
□visiting hours 面会時間
□vitamins ビタミン剤
□vomit 動 吐く
= throw up

W

□waist 腰
□weigh 動 ～の重さをはかる
□weight 名 体重
lose weight 体重が減る
put on（= gain）weight 体重が増える
□wheelchair 車椅子
□white blood cell 白血球
□WHO（World Health Organization）世界保健機構
□wound 動 傷，～を傷つける
be wounded in ～で負傷する
□wrist 手首

X

□X-rays エックス線，レントゲン写真
an X-ray examination エックス線検査

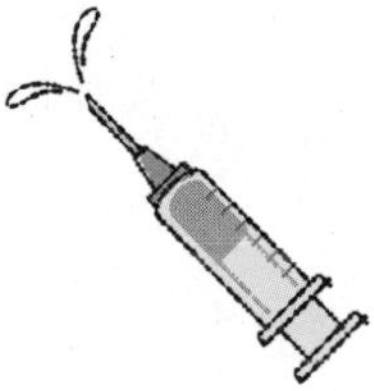

石原式　会話で攻略！　メディカルイングリッシュ

著　者　石原　修
発行人　竹田允彦
発行所　株式会社　キプリ
〒160-0022　東京都新宿区新宿2-14-6
発売元　株式会社　東京コア
〒160-0022　東京都新宿区新宿2-13-10
イラスト　小野寺美恵
印　刷　恵友印刷株式会社

定価はカバーに表示されています。乱丁本・落丁本はお取替えいたします。

ISBN978-4-924936-11-9 C7082